PRACTICAL TURKEY
HUNTING STRATEGIES

PRACTICAL TURKEY HUNTING STRATEGIES

How to Hunt Effectively Under Any Conditions

RAY EYE

The Lyons Press
Guilford, CT
An imprint of The Globe Pequot Press

The Lyons Press is an imprint of The Globe Pequot Press.

10 9 8 7 6 5 4
ISBN: 978-1-58574-875-4
Printed in the United States of America

Design by Compset, Inc.

Library of Congress Cataloging-in-Publication Data

Eye, Ray, 1952-
        Practical turkey hunting strategies: how to effectively hunt birds under any conditions / Ray Eye.
        p. cm.
Originally published: Hunting wild turkeys with Ray Eye / Michael Pearce. 1st ed. Harrisburg, Pa. : Stackpole Books, 1990.
ISBN 1-58574-875-7 (pbk. : alk. paper)
1. Turkey Hunting. I. Pearce, Michael, 1958- Hunting wild turkeys with Ray Eye. II. Title.

SK325. T8P43 2003
799.2'4645—dc21
2002043310

To buy books in quantity for corporate use
or incentives, call **(800) 962–0973**
or e-mail **premiums@GlobePequot.com.**

DEDICATION

This book is dedicated to the wild turkey.

ACKNOWLEDGMENTS

It would be impossible to thank everyone who has helped, inspired, or assisted in some way or another to help make the completion of this book a reality.

First and foremost I thank my wife Jan, my best friend and devoted mother of our wonderful children, Sara, Shane, and David.

My caring and loving Mom and Dad, who introduced me to the wonderful world of hunting and instilled in me the proper respect for both firearms and wildlife.

My Dad taught me the ways of the woods and became my favorite hunting partner. Mom and Dad always gave me support and encouragement, but most of all, gave me the ultimate gift of all, their time, precious time from working to earn a living to feed and raise five kids. They cared enough to make time to take me hunting.

My brother Marty, the finest turkey hunter I know, with turkey hunting and calling skills second to none. Marty's passion and love for turkey hunting is an inspiration to each and everyone he shares the woods with.

Last but not least, those very special people I have shared turkey hunts and campfires with for many years. In a way they too are family: Gerald Bethge, Pat Leonard, Rick Story, Mike Held, and Ralph Duren.

Again, it is impossible to list everyone, like the many outdoor writers who told my story and supported me for so many years: Gerald Bethge, Mike Pearce, Tom Huggler, John Phillips, and Ralph Stuart. There are just too many to mention. To each and every one of you, I thank you from the bottom of my heart.

CONTENTS

INTRODUCTION

In the mid-1960s, while turkey hunting Johnston Mountain in the Missouri Ozarks, I set up on a gobbling turkey with my grandpa's gun stuck through a split-rail fence made by my great-great grandpa. Little did I realize at the time that someday, in future years, I would hunt all subspecies of the wild turkey throughout this great country, including the Hawaiian Islands.

During those early years there was little or no information available on turkey hunting. Successful turkey hunters were very secretive, and would rarely share information about their hunting techniques. I learned from trial and error and the wild turkey itself. Hunters used homemade calls or their voices to lure gobblers into range. A shotgun was used to hunt everything year round, and shells were whatever was left over from the fall.

Today's turkey hunters are very fortunate to have a wealth of solid, helpful information available to them: videos, magazines, seminars, and books such as this one. There are also great products to help them hunt effectively: specialized turkey guns, turkey loads, camouflage clothing, decoys, ATVs, and modern turkey calls

From Johnston Mountain to hunting full time, doing a radio show, writing magazine articles and books, conducting seminars, and taping videos and television shows, I am blessed and very fortunate to make a living turkey hunting. I know that turning a passion into your job is not something many people have the opportunity to do.

Now I have the opportunity once more to share with you what I have learned during some forty years of turkey hunting. I made as many mistakes as anyone, but that is how we all learn, and yes, I am still learning every time I hunt.

I hope that somewhere within this book, you will read something that will help you to enjoy a fun, safe, and successful turkey hunt. Tactics within these pages have served me well, and I have enjoyed many successful turkey hunts. In addition, I do not believe there is just one particular way to hunt wild turkeys. A turkey hunter should be willing to change and adapt to any hunting situation, weather conditions, terrain, and the cycle of the wild turkey at the time of the hunt.

I am honored, privileged, and fortunate to be a spokesperson for turkey hunting and the great outdoors. I appreciate the opportunity to share with you, a fellow turkey hunter, this book full of years of trials and tribulations of my turkey hunting career. Read with an open mind, thinking about your experiences and how they may relate. The book will give you guidelines, but all hunters should form their own opinions, use common sense, and learn from the best teacher of all, the wild turkey.

Ray Eye
December 15, 2002

1

THE EARLY YEARS

My grandfather took one last sip of coffee, pushed his breakfast plate aside, and stood as he pulled out his pocketwatch. Opening the lid of the old timepiece, he said, "You'd better be going, boy, if you want to kill turkey."

His words caught me off guard, so much so that it was several seconds before I could stammer a reply. "But Pop, aren't you going with me . . . ? I've never been turkey hunting before."

"I'd like to, Ray, but you know I've got chores to do," he answered, putting a hand on my shoulder. "Besides, the only way you're really going to learn is to get up there and do it by yourself. Now come on, you'd better get going."

I stood there in a state of shock and watched the old man leave the room to get his trusted Winchester 97 and a handful of shells. Following him to the back door, I still couldn't believe what was happening.

Just outside the door he reached up and took down a kerosene lantern, scratched a match against its base, lit it, and handed it to me. "You know where to go on the mountain and what to do, boy. God knows we've been through it enough," he said as he stuffed the shotgun shell into my faded bib overalls. "Just remember what I've told you and be careful." He placed the shotgun in my other hand and gave me a pat on the back that nudged me on my way.

Holding the lantern high I headed across the yard, now more scared than excited. Those first few steps that I took as a nine-year-old were the toughest I'd ever taken—or would ever take.

Some of my first memories are of the weekends spent on my grandparents' farm deep in the Missouri Ozarks. Located three miles up a valley, or "holler" as they call it in the hills, the farm had been the home of three generations in my family.

The white, two-story farmhouse was typical for the hills. A clear, spring-fed creek ran only a few yards from the front door, past the barn and other outbuildings. The house sat in a rare Ozark meadow, surrounded on three sides by steep evergreen- and hardwood-covered hills. The highest of the hills was simply referred to as "the mountain" because it was one of the highest points in the state.

In 1962, the year I headed up the mountain that dark morning, most of America was in the middle of a rapid modernization. Not so in the backcountry around the farm. Life had changed little since my dad was born in the house decades before.

Electricity had just arrived, but indoor plumbing hadn't, and the telephone never did. The roads were a far cry from what most Americans were used to. During the spring, the dirt path leading to Grandpa's turned into a muddy trough.

But there were advantages to living such a life. For one thing, it was simple. Everything was hard work, and you did the best you could with what was at hand. Also, there was a closeness between family and friends that sometimes slips away with progress.

The primitivism of the mountains made them sanctuaries for wildlife. Small game was abundant, and deer and turkeys had never been pushed or shot out of the rough backcountry. Hunting was a way of life, as much a means of putting food on the table as it was recreation. Like previous generations, I was educated at an early age. I listened to men tell old hunting tales and tagged along on squirrel hunts before I was five.

I loved it all, but turkeys held a particular fascination. They seemed to possess an almost mystical quality. They were rarely seen but always there. I can remember one spring morning like yesterday. Black storm clouds were marching over the mountain, and Pop and I were hurrying to get the last of the chores done.

With the first rumble of thunder came a gobble from a nearby ridge, then another and another. I stood there, my mouth hanging open in amazement as the hills around the farm came alive with gobbles. Pop finally snapped me out of my trance, and we made it to the house just as the first of the big raindrops banged down on the tin roof.

As a youngster, I had turkeys on my mind constantly. In the woods I was always looking for turkeys and I always asked my dad to explain any kind of evidence of their presence. I badgered poor Grandpa relentlessly, asking him to retell stories about turkey hunting when he was young. Looking back, I now realize he showed a great deal of patience and answered most questions to my satisfaction. Except for one: "When will I be old enough to hunt turkeys?" "Someday" was his standard answer.

One fall day his answer changed. The smell of homemade bread was in the air as we cut wood for the cookstove. Pausing to watch me work, Pop smiled and said out of the blue, "Ray, I think you'll be big enough by next spring." He didn't need to explain; I knew exactly what he meant.

A little later he gave me what became my most prized possession—my own turkey call. Grandpa had made it by hand, using a piece of slate from the chalkboard at an old one-room schoolhouse. For a striker he'd cut a piece of cedar from a fence post and fit it in the bottom of a hollowed-out corncob.

The call was my life, and I practiced religiously. Teachers took the call away from me more than once for using it at school.

Grandma said I sounded like "a cat caught in a fence," and Pop kept telling me to keep practicing.

The winter of 1961–62 was the longest of my life, but it eventually ended. Turkey season was only a week away when Pop shook me awake one cold April morning and said, "Get up. We're going up on the mountain for a while."

I did my best to keep up with him in the predawn darkness as we crossed the creek, headed across the dew-covered pasture, and found the old trail that would take us up the mountain. We walked quietly until we came to a huge oak at the junction of two ridges.

I started to ask one of the dozens of questions that were floating in my mind, but Grandpa quickly silenced me with a finger to his lips. Cupping his hands around his mouth, he let loose an imitation of a barred owl. Imagine how I felt when a turkey gobbled down the ridge to the northwest.

We stood there for a while and listened to the sounds of turkeys gobbling all over the hills. Each time one called, the bird in front of us rifled back a reply.

As we turned to leave, Pop whispered, "This is the place, boy. You'll want to sit with your back against that big oak, facing down that ridge. Use your call and whatever you do, don't move until you're ready to come home."

I was a bundle of nerves and anticipation the night before my hunt. Hoping to make the next day arrive faster, I slipped into bed after supper, already wearing my hunting clothes, except for my oversized work jacket and old tennis shoes.

Sleep was slow to come. I lay in bed listening to the calls of the whippoorwills, the coyotes yipping on the mountain, and the steady sound of the stream flowing nearby. I'd been awake for hours when the smell of homemade biscuits and frying bacon and eggs drifted upstairs.

Normally I'd have devoured the breakfast in front of me in a matter of minutes, but not that morning. I picked at the meal and never took my eyes off Grandpa.

When he broke the news that I'd be hunting alone I was heart-broken. For years I'd pictured us hunting together. The thought of trying for one of the mountain's phantom birds alone was beyond my young imagination.

I tried to present myself as a man as I headed toward the creek. In some ways today brought the realization of a lifelong dream. I was going up on the mountain to try to kill a turkey. The fact that I was carrying Grandpa's favorite shotgun was an accomplishment. But inside I was as scared as I'd ever been.

My hands full, I had trouble crossing the stream. Midway across I missed a steppingstone and ended up knee-deep in cold water. I made my way across the pasture, wet shoes squeaking with every step.

I'd walked the trail to the top of the mountain dozens of times, but never had it seemed so long or so frightening. I finally arrived at the big oak, put out the lantern, and sat down.

I strained to remember everything Grandpa had told me as I quietly slipped the blue paper shells into the pump gun. I sat there shivering from both cold and fear, desperately hoping Pop would come walking up the trail.

With the reddening of the eastern horizon came the sounds of life in the timber. At first I heard only songbirds, and I began to relax a little. Then came the eight-note call of a barred owl. I caught my breath when the turkey gobbled from down the ridge.

I picked up the slate call but couldn't use it. I was afraid, afraid I'd goof up and scare the turkey and ruin my dream. Again and again I tried to rub the cedar against the slate but each time I pulled back. Finally I shut my eyes, swallowed the huge lump in my throat and shakingly rubbed the peg against the call. I winced at the gosh-awful noise it produced.

Whether it was in response to my call or just coincidence I'll never know, but the gobbler sounded off. Several more times I tried to force some yelps from the call but couldn't. I finally dropped the call in frustration and clutched the gun that was resting on my knees.

By then I could hear turkeys gobbling all around me, the closest two being the bird in front of me and a tom on the next ridge. I waited and listened to the birds gobbling; I could tell they were not moving.

Suddenly came the soft yelps of a hen turkey behind me. I began to panic, fearing the hen would call the gobblers away from me. I started to get up to move closer to the hen but suddenly I remembered Pop saying, "Whatever you do, don't move. . ." Even though it looked hopeless, I stayed.

Soon the three birds were calling almost nonstop, and the two gobblers were headed my way. Then I realized that the hen was actually a blessing. To get to her the gobblers would have to walk right past me. Since I was too nervous to call, she was my only hope.

I could hear the two toms getting closer to each other but wasn't prepared for what came next. From just below the ridge came the loud noises of deep turkey purrs, flapping wings, and feathered bodies thumping together.

I didn't know it then, but the two birds were fighting for the hen. I was shaking so hard I thought for sure the turkeys would see me, and the end of the gun barrel was drawing circles the size of doughnuts.

Hearing the sounds of tree limbs breaking, I watched a big turkey rise through the trees and sail out across the valley. A loud, triumphant gobble sounded from the scene of the battle, and the hen responded with a series of clucks and yelps. My pounding heart went into overdrive. Breathing was hard, and my black-rimmed glasses started to fog.

The next time the tom sounded off he was so close I could hear a rattle in his gobble. Like a ghost, he suddenly appeared to my right, head tucked back, feathers puffed out, and wings dragging the ground.

My first impulse was to swing the gun and shoot, but in the back of my mind I heard Pop stressing, "Never move a muscle when you can see the turkey's head. If you do he'll spot you for sure. And remember to aim just for the head."

Seconds seemed like hours, but I waited. When the bird stepped behind a big hickory I twisted my body, cocked the hammer, and raised the gun. There was a deafening boom as the old gun went off when the turkey stepped back into view. In my haste I'd tucked the stock under my arm, and the old Winchester had shot up and struck me in the face, bloodying my nose and sending my glasses flying.

Holding onto the gun with one hand I rummaged through the leaves, found my broken glasses, and poked them on my face as I ran to where I'd last seen the bird. My foot caught a root and I tumbled down the ridge. When I finally stopped rolling I looked up and there he was, stretched out, his feathers glistening in the sun.

I arrived down at the farm, soaking wet, covered with mud and blood, half dragging and half carrying a turkey that weighed half as much as I did. Grandpa heard my shouts and was waiting for me.

He admired the bird, congratulated me, and then laughingly said, "You'd better run along and get yourself cleaned up before your grandma has a fit." I spent the rest of the day telling and re-telling him how I'd killed the big gobbler, fibbing a little by explaining how I'd called the bird myself. He smiled and listened to every word.

A lot's changed since then. My life has never been the same. After I took that turkey, I was in the woods calling every spare minute I had. It cost me girlfriends, it cost me jobs, and it almost got me kicked out of school several times. But it was an addiction I wouldn't have cured if I could have.

I learned a lot about calling turkeys that April morning, and I've learned a lot since. In fact I've learned enough to make my living at it. I present seminars all across America, appear on many videos, have an outdoor radio show, hunt on television, and pro-staff for many great companies.

Grandpa and Grandma had to move off the farm and into a small community nearby. We lost Grandpa in 1976, and Grandma continued to tease me about sounding like "a cat caught in a fence."

It wasn't long after Grandpa passed away that the entire family was gathered at Grandma's. As usual, the talk turned to hunting, and someone brought up the subject of my first turkey. My eyes began to moisten and I walked over and leaned against the fence to look out towards the mountain that held so many fond memories of Pop.

A few seconds later I felt Grandma's hand rub my shoulder softly as she said, "You're thinking of Pop, aren't you?" Never taking my eyes off the mountain, I bit my lip and nodded my head.

She lovingly moved in beside me and softly said, "Ray, do you remember that hen on the mountain the morning you killed your first turkey?"

I looked at her, swallowed hard, and said, "Yes."

"That wasn't a hen calling behind you," she said, "that was your Grandpa."

2

WILD TURKEY HABITAT AND DISTRIBUTION

No one knows for sure how long the gobble of the wild turkey has echoed across what is now called America. Archeological digs have shown that native Americans used turkeys for a variety of purposes for thousands of years before the first European explorer saw his first turkey.

Turkeys thrived for centuries, occupying a range that covered roughly the eastern half of the country and much of the Southwest. Some estimate that the population may have reached eight to ten million.

The earliest settlers found the birds not only abundant, but easily harvested and popular on the table. Unfortunately they were a little too popular. By the early part of the twentieth century, loss of habitat, baiting, roost-shooting, and other means of slaughtering turkeys had significantly reduced their numbers.

The gobble of the wild turkey was largely limited to a few scattered pockets of wilderness. Some predicted that the bird would follow the path of the endangered buffalo, and possibly the extinct passenger pigeon.

But with the advent of modern game management, the hope was for turkeys not only to survive but to possibly recapture some of their original range. The turkeys' comeback has no doubt surpassed the wildest dreams of those who first trapped and transplanted turkeys in the 1940s and 1950s.

The springtime calls of gobblers and hens can now be heard in every state except Alaska. Turkeys are thriving even in states where they were historically absent.

State game departments deserve much of the credit, as do conservation organizations like the National Wild Turkey Federation. Yet the birds themselves deserve most of the credit. Given a chance, wild turkeys waste little time taking a foothold.

Wild turkey hens have a natural ability to pull off huge clutches and hatches to fill underutilized habitat. Releases of three toms and nine hens have grown to estimated flocks of hundreds of turkeys in as little as five years.

An adult gobbler's head and neck. Compared to the hen, the gobbler is usually larger in size and has more coloration of red, white, and blue. But the best identification is always a visible beard.

Flocks have also expanded to, and are thriving in, habitat that was thought to be unsuitable as recently as the early 1990s.

Wild turkeys thrive in as wide a range of habitat as any game-bird in the United States, from the desert lowlands to the swamps of Florida and the pine-covered ridges of the Rocky Mountains.

Through the centuries turkeys learned to adapt to their environments, developing into several recognizable subspecies. The four common in the United States are the eastern, Merriam's, Rio Grande, and Florida, or Osceola.

Some hunters talk as if the four were almost distinct species. In truth they have far more in common than not. They all possess the eyes of an eagle, the ears of a white-tailed deer, and the paranoia of a coyote.

There may be some debate about the ease of harvesting the various turkeys. Many eastern hunters have returned from prairie hunts with tales of quick success and "stupid" gobblers.

But it's my experience that the higher success rates on western turkeys have more to do with the amount of habitat, current conditions, and hunting pressure. Heavily hunted Rio Grandes have rattled my confidence during an unusually late spring. Farmland easterns, if they had very little hunting pressure, were nearly impossible to spook after they came to calls.

All subspecies are more adaptable than commonly believed. Historically the Rio Grande was found throughout western Texas and up into southern Oklahoma. Now this bird is common as far north as Kansas and Nebraska. Early explorer and naturalist accounts show that the eastern, known as the noble turkey of the hardwood forests, was the original turkey on the plains of Kansas and Oklahoma.

The four subspecies have enough in common that they interbreed. In fact, interbreeding is often encouraged. Terry Funk, a Kansas turkey biologist, tells how the northwestern part of his state was once occupied by a stagnating flock of Rio Grandes. A few eastern toms were released in the land of mule deer and prairie dogs. The easterns not only survived, but created a virtual population explosion. Intentional stockings of eastern toms and Rio Grande hens have flourished in other places as well.

No matter which bird you hunt, they all have a way of doubling your pulse and electrifying your nerves. They each possess their own special way of making even the most experienced hunter feel like a rank amateur.

EASTERN

The most populous and well known are the eastern turkeys. They occupy a range from northern Florida to Maine, and from the Atlantic seaboard to central Kansas. Often heavily hunted in a seemingly endless sea of habitat, with pressure easterns are possibly the most challenging of all turkeys.

The eastern wild turkey is the most common of all subspecies.

OSCEOLA

One of the toughest aspects of bagging Osceolas is simply getting a chance to hunt them. Found only in parts of Florida, Osceolas are far from pushovers. As with turkey hunting in other parts of the South, the swamps that these gobblers so love can make for challenging, and often very wet, hunting.

MERRIAM'S

The turkeys of the western United States, Merriam's often come readily to calls, but a lack of understory in their habitat makes it difficult for the hunter to remain hidden long enough to bag this bird. These turkeys always sound farther away than they really are. There are good populations of this bird on public ground. The Black Hills of South Dakota alone offer close to a million acres of Merriam's hunting. Scouting can be as important as it is with easterns.

RIO GRANDE

Often living in limited habitat, Rio Grandes in Texas, Oklahoma, and Kansas offer the highest success rates for hunters of the four subspecies. But the open terrain can work in favor of the sharp-eyed birds as well.

Sneaking into a calling site can take some planning and effort. Hunters must be well concealed and must remain perfectly still.

TROPHIES

Interestingly enough, each of the four subspecies has its advantages over the others. The Osceolas, obviously, are the rarest and will have some impressive spurs. Easterns tend to be bigger in beard length and body size.

The ivory tips on the back and tail feathers make Merriam's the most beautiful. The light coloring of the Rio Grandes makes them a close second to the Merriam's in terms of looks. But my favorite char-

The spur on the leg of the male is the way to age the wild turkey gobbler. The longer the spur, the older the bird.

acteristic of the dryland turkeys is their open habitat, which sometimes makes it possible to watch the bird work for hundreds of yards.

One common denominator for comparing the quality of birds is spur length. Tag a bird that can be hung on a tree limb by his spurs and you've taken one of America's finest trophies, whether he's a sixteen-pound Texas Rio Grande or a twenty-six-pound Iowa eastern.

A TURKEY'S LIFE CYCLE

For close to four weeks, the hen sits beneath the little tangle of briers. She had previously come for only a short while each day, depositing an egg or two onto the leaves, then departing.

Though there are no absolutes in wildlife, the hen probably laid an average clutch of twelve, and with the final egg her vigil began. The three-year-old hen could sit nearly motionless for hours, leaving her nest only to pick a few bugs or greens and to get a quick drink from the nearby stream.

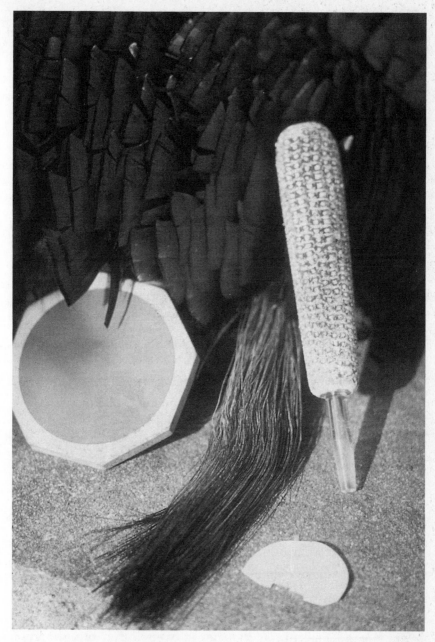

Close-up of an adult gobbler's beard. The beard is actually a primitive feather. Beard lengths vary according to habitat. Older birds often have longer beards, but beard length is not an accurate measure of a turkey's age.

James Hall with an Osceola taken in south Florida.

And so far she has been lucky. A nest at the other end of the overgrown field had been discovered and demolished by a raccoon. Other nests in the area had been destroyed by farm machinery, or raided by skunks and a host of other animals.

The previous year her first clutch had met a similar fate. The old hen had been forced to re-nest and try again, with a smaller number of eggs.

On the twenty-eighth day of her wait the eggs begin to pop apart and the small, two-inch chicks step into the world. Soon ten of the dozen eggs had hatched. For a reason known only to nature, the other pair never would.

In a matter of hours the hen's life changes from one of peace to seeming pandemonium as she tries to oversee the young turkeys. The day-old poults can walk amazingly well as they follow the hen. Like the bigger bird, they instinctively search for and eat insects.

Bob Sarber took this beautiful Merriam's in New Mexico on a hunt with the author.

Preyed upon by almost everything with teeth and talons, the young turkeys transform the hen into the ultimate paranoid. At the first sign of danger the hen sounds an alarm putt that makes the mottled brown chicks squat and freeze, easily blending in with their surroundings.

Like most wildlife, the hen displays amazing bravery when defending her young. Twice she fakes a broken wing to lead a coyote away from her hiding brood. Still, the brood is gradually shrinking in number.

Her job becomes easier with the turkeys' rapid growth. By the start of their third week the poults begin to get airborne and can roost on low-hanging limbs and bushes.

Food is abundant, seemingly limitless. The hen and poults spend a lot of time in a nearby farm field, picking up grasshoppers and other insects that were munching on the crops. Like the hen, the poults will eat almost anything they can get in their mouths: greens, seeds, and maybe an occasional small lizard from a rock pile or crawfish from the shallow stream.

With the coming of autumn, the remaining young—two hens and a tom—are two-thirds the size of the hen. They still follow her as she feeds in the hardwoods, using their big feet to move the leaves that mask an assortment of wild nuts and insects.

As the days shorten and the weather cools, the hen and her young begin to mix in with similar flocks. Midwinter finds the flock concentrated around a harvested soybean field which, along with nearby acorns, provides their main source of food. Their feathers offer plenty of insulation from the cold. As long as they can reach food they will survive the winter.

A growing excitement spreads through the flock as spring approaches. The turkeys start to disperse, and the toms begin to gobble and have shoving matches to establish their places in the pecking order.

A veteran from springs past, the old hen takes the changes in stride. Her two female offspring are a little confused, but their befuddlement is minor compared to the mixed-up feelings of the young tom.

Now bigger than his mother, the jake basically looks the part of a tom. Unlike the dull brown of a hen, his feathers are black-tipped and shiny. Though rounded and dull, small spurs sprout from the backs of his legs. From his chest protrudes a stubby, primitive feather known as a beard.

The young tom, called a jake, is at the awkward age of adolescence when hormones are raging through his young body but he's not totally sure what to do. Occasionally he gets so excited that he raises his body feathers, fans his uneven tail, and maybe even cuts loose with a broken gobble.

Yet all too often his theatrics only get him in trouble. The bigger gobblers that tolerated him in the winter seem to take no greater pleasure than knocking the stuffing out of the smaller jake whenever he shows any signs of bravado.

He eventually mixes in with three of his own kind. Low birds on the totem pole, they mostly watch the spring ritual of replenishment from a distance. Once a hen lowers herself in front of the most dominant of the four. Another time they throw all caution aside and run to the calls of an unseen hen. The small flock is down to three after the loud bang rolls across the countryside.

The jake has it easy throughout the summer, obtaining food in much the same manner he did the year before as a poult. His body and features continue to fill out as autumn and then winter arrive. A full-fledged adult, the tom has few natural enemies, but persists in the paranoia that his mother taught him. The sights and sounds of people in his woods naturally seem to terrify him the most.

He spends the winter with several of his long-bearded counterparts. The ever-present pecking order keeps each bird in his place,

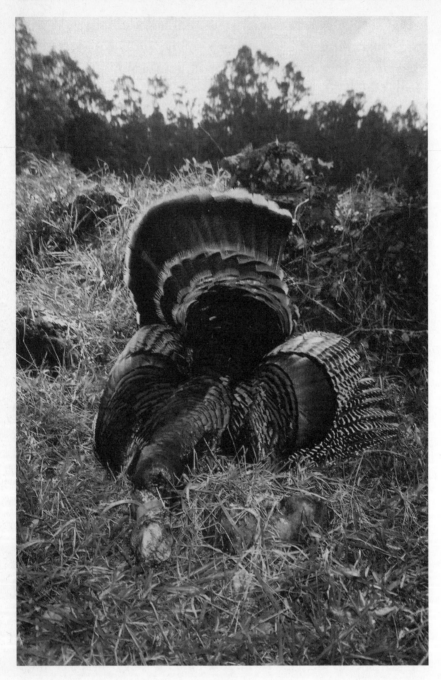

The white-tipped back and tail feathers make the Rio Grande one of the prettiest turkeys.

yet they get along well. That is, they do until the combination of lengthening daylight and warm temperatures again begins to fill their minds with thoughts of love.

The toms become more and more agitated with each other's presence. Gobblers begin to challenge gobblers, and fights are common.

From a distance it's tough to distinguish the two-year-old bird from older toms. His body is almost as large as theirs, as is his beard. Unlike the year before, he spends more time standing his ground and less time running.

The bird can hold his own against most two-year-old and some three-year-old gobblers, but he's no match for a couple of the real monarchs that rule the area. His spurs are three-quarters of an inch,

Some gobblers have more than one beard. This is a multi-bearded Illinois gobbler taken by Mike Weller.

Hunting typical south Texas Rio Grande country.

and pointed but not terribly sharp, no match for the 1¼-inch curved spikes of the four- and five-year-olds.

That spring he scrounges a few hens to breed. The next year, the bird's third, is much better. He is one of the dominant birds in the pecking order, one that can be bullied by only a few other toms. He has his own little territory, and many chicks come into the world carrying his genes.

As a four-year-old, the tom is the boss bird. Shortly after the winter flocks break up, he settles the matter with another big gobbler. The two close in on each other, gobbling challenges as they approach.

They bump bodies, flog each other, and wrap their necks together in a tug of war. They also rise into the air time and time again, slashing at each other with their razor-sharp spurs. Finally the

Eastern wild turkey nest. Gobbler hunting in the spring is best when most of the hens are on the nest.

other gobbler retreats, and the tom enjoys the best that the area has to offer—the best habitat and the most hens.

For a while the big gobbler is in the company of hens nearly all the time. There are hens with him when he flies from his morning roost and even more come to his gobbles throughout the day.

And then his life slowly begins to change. The hens begin nesting and the still hot tom spends more and more time looking for new loves.

The gobbler is strutting in his favorite meadow one morning. The single hen that was with him at daybreak has gone to her nest, and the tom is on his own.

On edge and excited, he gobbles at the sound of an owl hoot in the distance. Then, from up on the ridge, come the sweet calls of a hen. He first hears a few soft clucks and gentle yelps. The tom gobbles back, expecting the hen to come to him. But she doesn't, and the next series of yelps comes from the same area.

The tom stands his ground for a while, but a string of excited cutting and yelping is more than he can stand. He takes his time moving toward the hen, still expecting her to come running like all the rest.

The old patriarch stops often to strut, only to be coaxed onward by seductive promises. As he nears, the bird's ears pinpoint the source of the calls just over the lip of the ridge in front of him.

The tom steps over the break, showing his finest strut. A soft putt pulls him from strut and he raises his head to look for the unseen hen that's been leading him on. . .

3

SOUNDS TURKEYS MAKE

Turkey hunting has an almost magical allure for those who do it. Calling seems to be one of the prime attractions. Hunting a species that the hunter basically talks to, and it answers, then responds by moving closer and closer is not for the faint of heart.

Turkeys are very vocal and spend a lot of time communicating with each other. Granted, it may not be a language, but there are certain sounds that mean certain things. The better hunters understand the calls, the more they understand turkeys and what it takes to get in on the conversation.

There's no way I can really explain the sounds of wild turkeys in this book. What I can do, however, is take a little time to explain their system of communication.

HENS

YELP

The yelp is unquestionably the most universal of all turkey sounds, yet it's also the call that has the greatest amount of variance.

Though the basic call sounds like the word "calk" or "keowk," hens use yelps as the basis of a wide variety of calls. In my opinion, the way the yelp is expressed gives the call its true meaning.

For instance, hens often use really soft, low yelps to convey a sense of security. They yelp like this when feeding, when waking up on the roost in the morning (commonly known as tree yelping), and in just about any other situation when things are calm.

But the yelps sound totally different when the hen is trying to express some excitement—such as when she wants to mate in the worst sort of way. Wild turkey hens put feeling and inflection in their yelps. Turkeys call depending on how they feel at the time and the circumstances. The tone, length, and amount of rasp during yelping depend on the mood. Wild hens may begin yelping clear, short yelps, then build in length and volume into loud, raspy yelping.

The mating yelp is a call that's often full of excitement and desire. It's definitely louder than the soft yelps of contentment. The degree of excitement and the length of the mating call vary not only from bird to bird, but also from time to time.

No two turkeys sound or call alike. Some say that a mating yelp numbers three to six yelps, and should be made every eight minutes Remember, turkeys do not count or wear watches.

I've heard hens going to a gobbler putting no more than two or three yelps together. On the same ridge I've heard a hen yelp nonstop as she runs to a gobbler.

Hens often use yelps for locating each other. Again, how they feel determines how they sound. If they want only to check in with another bird they may sound just a couple of unexcited yelps.

If they've been separated from other turkeys from their group they're trying to find, you will often hear the panic in their long string of yelps. Likewise, you can hear the anger in the yelps of a dominant hen that's flustered, with a bird challenging her place at the top of the pecking order.

CLUCK

Like the soft yelp, the short and soft cluck is a basic call of contentment. Hens use it to keep track of each other, hut I've heard lone hens clucking as if they're just trying to reassure themselves.

As with the yelp, the number of consecutive clucks varies from bird to bird and from circumstance to circumstance. Hens often cluck to communicate a feeling of ease with nearby turkeys. A feeding hen may cluck only once or twice, while a hen caught deep in the grasp of passion may cluck fast and almost continuously to the gobbler that's courting her.

PUTT

Many people associate putting with alarmed turkeys, but turkeys will putt, or "pop" as some call it, under a variety of conditions. They may start putting loudly when they're spooked, but they can make the same sounds when they're excited for other reasons, like anger or pleasure.

CACKLE

Most of the cackling I've heard is during the morning fly-down from the roost. The cackle begins with clucking, then rises into excited putting and cutting on the way to the ground.

CUTTING

Cutting is a string of very aggressive and usually loud putting. Cutting is my most used call for calling and killing turkeys. Its rhythm is fast and full of excitement. Cutting mixed with yelping adds incredible realism. Hens often cut as they're flying off the roost in the morning and when they're getting impatient trying to find a gobbler. A hen that's challenging another hen for placement in the pecking order can also do a lot of excited cutting.

PURRS

A rolling, almost vibrating call, purring usually means contentment. It is soft communication. Like most calls it can be long and drawn out or short and quick. Feeding hens often purr as they peck at food. Sometimes the purring is so soft hunters can't hear it unless they're within twenty or thirty yards.

But as with most calls, purring can also be loud and sometimes aggressive. Hens often purr a lot when they've been separated and are trying to regroup.

Two hens getting ready to settle a dispute—over their places in the pecking order or anything else—can start purring hard, long, and loud as their excitement builds.

KEE-KEE

The kee-kee is the real lost call of the wild turkeys. Almost the only time you hear the whistling kee-kee is when turkeys are trying to regroup. This call is almost always full of excitement and often panic as the birds hurry to find each other.

ALL OF THE ABOVE

As you can tell, there isn't any one call that precisely expresses whatever a turkey is trying to communicate. An excited hen might yelp, putt, cut, and purr to get a gobbler's attention. Chances are she'll make a combination of two or more calls to get her point across.

Those who have listened to real hens excitedly calling to gobblers will tell you that it's rare for a hen to simply yelp. A hen's calls often change as the excitement builds.

For instance, a hen may start off with a few clucks or mellow yelps when she's looking for a tom. When she gets a response her yelps may become snappier in rhythm, louder, and longer. As time passes and her agitation increases, she may send out a string of excited cuts and a few enthusiastic yelps. She may eventually forget all about the yelps and use nothing but cutting.

On the other hand, another hen may stick mainly to yelps while filling in with some soothing clucks and purrs to find a tom. No two turkeys call alike.

TOMS

GOBBLE

A tom's gobble is the most exhilarating and misunderstood of all turkey calls. While wild turkeys gobble with much more intensity during the spring mating season, the gobble is the male's most aggressive vocalization and is used throughout the year

The gobble is a call of pure excitement and intensity. I've heard it all twelve months of the year. In the fall the gobble can be a

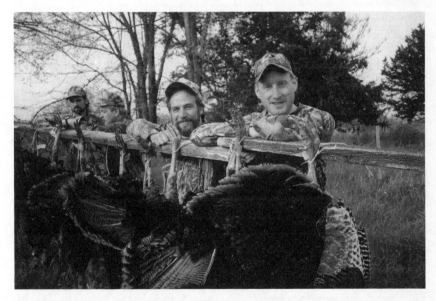

Successful hunters with their birds. Each bird responded differently, coming in to a variety of yelps, cackles, clucks, and putts.

gathering call for a dispersed flock of mature bachelor longbeards, or for dominance in the pecking order. Any time of year it is a sign of excitement and the sound that hunters live for.

Many years ago during a fall hunt, I watched a flock of eight gobblers trying to squeeze through a small hole in a woven wire fence. First one bird would try and then another. Eventually the birds started bumping into each other.

Soon I saw a tail fan out; minutes later a couple of birds began strutting to show their dominance. As the frenzy built, the toms began to gobble back and forth at each other. By the time it was over all eight birds were standing and gobbling at each other. They continued nonstop for close to twenty minutes.

The reason for gobbling in the spring is the breeding season and the time of the most excitement. Gobbling intensifies as the day length increases. Toms are gobbling back and forth as they jockey for their places in the pecking order. The gobble is also their gathering call to round up willing hens.

Often any hint of surprise or excitement can get a tom to fire off a gobble. The shrill calling of a crow, the deep hoots of an owl, and a clap of thunder are all regular sources of inspiration.

When the hormones are charging through a bird's body at full speed, who knows what he'll gobble at? I once hunted a big longbeard in a patch of hardwoods that wasn't far from a small country school. The kids were playing softball at midmorning. Even a half mile away I could follow the progress of the game by the loud, enthusiastic screams of the kids. Many times the shrieks that followed a hit would be answered with a resounding gobble.

And it's been my experience that toms will start gobbling at a young age. I've seen jakes—year-old toms—stand in one spot and gobble almost nonstop for close to an hour. I don't think even they know why they're doing it. I've also heard young-of-the-year birds doing their best gobble when they get excited or separated from the flock.

YELP AND OTHER CALLS

Many hunters are so infatuated with just the gobble of a tom that they either don't think about or simply forget the rest of the calls in the gobbler's vocabulary.

Gobblers yelp much the way hens do. Their yelps range from the soft sounds of contentment to the excited yelps of a fall bird inquiring about the new bird on the block.

Like the gobble, the yelp is part of the tom's vocabulary throughout the year. Even though it is most commonly associated with the fall and winter, I've had full-grown gobblers come in yelping to spring hen calls.

Jakes are especially notorious for yelping a reply in the spring. Sometimes the response is a string of pure yelps, but sometimes it may include both yelps and gobbles. It all depends on the bird and what he's feeling at the time.

Toms use clucks and soft putts to convey that they are at ease and to communicate with the other toms of their flock. Two toms ready to square off for a fight will make aggressive purrs and loud putts to communicate the feeling of pure aggressiveness and to challenge the other tom. Gobblers often use loud cutting to accomplish the same thing, as well as to announce their place in the pecking order.

Most of the time, the calls of a tom are slightly more drawn out and deeper in tone than those of a hen. But I've seen a big longbeard open his mouth and let out a string of yelps as clear and sweet as cold spring water. From a distance I would have sworn I was listening to a young hen.

Pardon the repetition, but each bird is different.

SPIT AND DRUM

Even though it's not exactly a call, there's one last gobbler sound that's important to hunting—what's known as the spit and drum of a strutting tom. It's normally heard from an approaching gobbler in the spring: a deep hum that in some ways sounds like a distant truck stuck in the mud. The closer the gobbler gets, the louder it sounds. This one noise does more for my pulse than any in turkey hunting.

The sounds are made when the gobbler snaps in and out of full strut. The sharp hiss of the spit and the low, vibrating sound of the drumming can be heard from a distance of up to sixty yards.

It can be a tough sound to describe, and many beginners have trouble hearing it. I often encourage new hunters to spend some time listening to tame turkeys strutting. Once you hear the spit and drum, you'll never forget it.

4

CALLING TURKEYS

As a boy I went to great lengths to learn how to talk with the turkeys. I'd belly-crawl through wet leaves and muck to get within hearing distance of a flock. I'd follow them all day and then go home and mimic them night and day.

Back in the early 1960s there weren't many turkey callers in the Ozarks who would share information about calling, but I made it my business to meet them all. Just hearing a rumor about somebody bagging a gobbler would have me begging for a ride to hear every last detail of the hunt, especially how the hunter called. I learned that the first step in calling a wild turkey is simply being able to sound like one. Time after time I'd hear a gobbler that had ignored my calls open up to the first calls of a wild hen. At the time I wanted to make those sounds more than anything else in the world.

Things are a lot easier for the novice turkey hunter these days. There are more turkeys in the woods to listen to. Or a hunter can take the easier route by watching videos or listening to tapes or CDs of turkey calling.

There's no better place to hear good calling than at a turkey calling contest. You will hear caller after caller giving his best shot at imitating nearly every sound in a turkey's vocabulary.

Some say that the stage and the woods are two different places, and I agree with that to a certain degree. In a contest you are calling to people, not turkeys. Calling contests will improve your calling skills, especially if you compete. Whether you're competing or just attending, other hunters and callers are more than willing to share a wealth of information with you.

It's been written that fancy calling has no place in the wild, and that the good woodsmanship of a local boy could best the skills of a world champion time after time. That I do not agree with. Combine really good calling with good woodsmanship and other hunting skills, and you have a combination that can't be beat.

Championship callers like Terry Rohm, Preston Pittman, Billy McCoy, Walter Parrott, Don Ship, and Paul Butski are also some of the best turkey hunters in the nation. They follow the spring seasons the way migrant workers follow ripening crops—and their harvest success rates in states they've never seen are outstanding. All of these well-known hunters will tell you that good calling is a large part of their success. They all encourage hunters to learn every call they can.

The last decade has seen a lot of change in the turkey woods. There are more hunters today, and turkeys are exposed to more human activity than ever before. There are times when you don't need to be an advanced or "champion" caller. If most of the hens are nesting, the weather fair, and the hunting pressure light, a few yelps and clucks may be all it takes.

But when the weather is off, hunters are behind every tree, or the hens are clinging nymphomaniacs, it will take good calling to work birds into range. I've seen good callers consistently take turkeys under different situations and weather conditions, while less experienced hunters with little calling skill emerge from the woods without success time and time again.

Ask a hundred different turkey hunters and you'll probably get a hundred different theories on calling. I'll be the first to admit that my ideas don't agree with what is gospel to some people. But I know what's worked for me and for the many turkey hunters I've taught down through the years.

One of the most important ideas to remember is that each turkey has its own feelings and personality. I've never seen any two turkeys act the same, nor have I ever found any calling methods that work all the time. You have to be able to recognize what it takes to turn on different turkeys in different situations.

In my second year of turkey hunting I came upon a magazine in my grandparents' outhouse that contained an article on turkey hunting. It said the only way to call in a gobbler was to yelp three times, wait ten minutes, yelp three more times, and so on.

The next morning I walked up to a ridge where I knew a gobbler roosted. At daybreak the tom gobbled, and I closed the distance. I pulled a watch out of one pocket, my call out of another, and made three yelps. The gobbler hammered back a gobble, but I sat silently and stared at the watch. After ten minutes I yelped three more times, and the bird started gobbling harder. Then from my left came the yelps and cuts of a real hen turkey.

The more she called, the more the tom gobbled. The more the tom gobbled, the more excited she became. Within minutes the hen was calling almost nonstop. The tom flew from the roost and ran right to the hen. That hen ran away with my gobbler, even before my ten minutes were up.

It was obvious: That gobbler liked his ladies loud and demanding. But you really won't know what a turkey wants until you spend some time feeling him out. I usually advise hunters to start off calling simple and short. If you make a couple of soft yelps, the bird runs in gobbling nonstop, and you have to shoot him off your leg, then obviously you didn't need anything else.

A good rule of thumb is to make your first series of calls very soft, then increase in intensity as needed. A turkey can hear even the softest tree yelps from an amazing distance if the woods are quiet in the early morning.

If a gobbler is either not responding or responding but not moving closer, then start increasing your intensity. Try a longer and louder string of yelps. If that doesn't work, add some cutting to your yelps. You may end up having to make long strings of excited cutting to get a bird to come in.

How often should you call? That's a good question, but one that's impossible to answer. Every calling situation is different. If you can keep a gobbler interested with well-spaced calls, then you may be able to stick with it and get him.

But I've always been an aggressive caller. There are times when pouring it on hot and heavy is the only way to bring a bird into range. My last Oklahoma hunt with Terry Funk coincided with some of the worst hunting conditions in history. The birds weren't in their normal hangouts, nor were they responding well to our calls, or to other turkeys for that matter.

Terry and I were working a river bottom when a tom gobbled at my cutting. Not sure where the bird was, I stayed in the thick tamaracks while Terry sat near the edge of the trees. My first series of yelps got no response, but by building to some serious cutting I got the gobbler to sound off and eventually come in. The longbeard finally glided across the tiny river, and I shot him as he came through the tamaracks.

Later in the afternoon we got another single response, but my yelps failed to get the turkey to sound off again. I eventually built to a series of about thirty excited yelps before I got another answer. But the bird still didn't seem to be getting any closer.

To make a long story short, the one turkey we were calling was part of a mixed flock of a few toms and a lot of hens that showed some interest in really excited cutting. So that's what I did—almost

During the early years of my turkey hunting, I went to great lengths to learn to talk to turkeys. To this day, I believe sounding like a turkey is very important.

Always keep your box call well chalked, and never touch the calling surfaces with your fingers.

nonstop cutting for about forty-five minutes. In turn, the turkeys yelped, cut, and gobbled with the same intensity.

The dominant gobbler gave us the slip, but Terry was able to drop a longbeard from the flock when it finally got within range. Try not to use the same exact call time after time. Vary it a yelp or two each time to make it more authentic. Try to convey a feeling in your calls. Try to become a turkey.

Here's an example: I'm in the woods and a gobbler responds to my owl hoot from about three hundred yards away. Depending on the terrain, I'll move to within about two hundred yards, set up, and let out a few soft clucks and yelps, suggesting, "I'm kind of lonely; is anybody out there?"

If the bird responds I'll move a little closer and use a few more yelps to imply a hen that's cutting the distance and saying, "I'd like to meet you, where are you at?"

That may be all it takes. If the gobbler acts as if he's coming in, I use the same basic call to say, "Glad you're coming to see me; come on in." But if the gobbler won't budge or shows some hesitation, I step up the yelps and perhaps preface them with excited putts implying, "I'm really wanting to get together . . . soon!"

If the tom shows a little more interest but is taking too much time coming in, I may start the next call with some good cutting followed by the yelps. I'm trying to say, "Come on up and see me, big boy . . . and *hurry!*"

If I think he's still not working fast enough, I may eventually end up using some very aggressive and excited cutting. Sorry, but we can't print what I'm promising the gobbler.

Take a little time to think over the situation when you're having trouble getting a turkey to gobble at or come to your calls. Sometimes one small variation can make a big difference.

Some hunters may say you call too loudly, but what is too loudly? Turkeys call depending on their mood or how they feel. Calling volume depends on the conditions, terrain, and time of day you are hunting. Extremely loud yelps and cutting work well in stiff winds, but also may be the only thing that works on calm days. You just never know, so try different calling techniques until something works.

One perfectly still morning before turkey hunting season I was walking a logging road while I worked on a troublesome mouth call. I gave a few soft yelps that were really just loud enough for me to hear well. A turkey gobbled from about three hundred yards away.

"What a coincidence," I thought. A minute or so later I tried the same call, and the same bird gobbled back. I waited a few minutes and called again. That time the gobble was closer.

Changing the mechanical call you're using can sometimes get a bird turned on, especially if your skill with a diaphragm call is limited and the area you're hunting has lots of pressure. Change positions on the bird, pull out a box or slate call, and you may have the bird eating out of your hand.

It was late morning after guiding earlier; I set out on my own to work a good turkey that lived in some heavily hunted timber. Knowing that most hunters were coming into the area from the east, I circled around to the west and set up away from roads and other hunters.

Using my box call, I gave three or four raspy yelps with an up-and-down kind of turkey rhythm, a sound that can only be duplicated on a good box call. A coarse gobble sounded out in front of me around 350 yards. After fifteen minutes or so I gave a similar call, and he was closer. Patience and the waiting game were in order for this heavily hunted area.

I played it soft and easy, calling only four times in the hour it took the bird to close the 350 yards between us. I took the 24½-pound gobbler at twenty yards. The old gobbler's longest spur measured 1¾ inches. In some situations it might be possible to call too much. At times a gobbler can get so worked up he will not come in. If that is the case after calling a lot, go silent for a time; the gobbler will sometimes come in silent looking for the hen he heard earlier.

Too many hunters concentrate only on calling from hen to gobbler. If the tom's not coming in, do some experimenting. He may have some lady friends; try some challenging hen calls. The pecking order of the hens can result in a strutting tom following the challenged hens to your gun.

If you can't get a gobbler interested in romance, maybe you can toss some insults at him. Make your calls raspier and more drawn-out—like those of another gobbler or jake. When the spring comes late and the toms are more concerned with dominance than mating, sounding like a smart aleck can really get on the nerves of a dominant longbeard.

The main thing to remember is to approach calling with an

Aggressive calling, cutting, and loud, nonstop yelping brought success to this New England Outdoor Writers camp.

open mind and to be prepared for anything. If the hunt isn't going well, try some of the more advanced calls, such as aggressive cutting and gobbler or jake yelps. You have nothing to lose, but much to gain.

And no doubt the best way to learn is to actually get out and call in turkeys. Use common sense. If you do some calling to locate turkeys before the season, do not walk through your hunting area. Activity will spook the birds, so call from a distance. In fact, it's probably best to call and simply listen the last week before the season. Calling after the season has ended is also good practice.

Be sure you don't go to the same place every day to call the turkeys, especially on public ground. Go often enough to get your confidence up, but again, use your common sense. If you still have a problem with calling prior to the season, just call and practice on birds where your buddies will hunt.

5

CALLS

I remember asking Grandpa over and over to tell me about his grandfather hunting turkeys back in Virginia, and then Grandpa would talk about his younger years when he hunted and called turkeys in the hills—to shoot and to feed the family. Throughout each story I'd beg him to repeat the very sounds he'd used to call turkeys to the gun.

Sometimes he'd call with his voice; other times he'd use a homemade slate call, an old piece of blackboard slate from an old one-room schoolhouse. The striker was a hollowed-out corncob with a stick whittled from a seasoned cedar fence post from the farm.

One of my favorite stories is how he chalked the stock of his old shotgun, then produced yelps and clucks by pulling a small wooden box striker with turkey rhythm along the old Winchester's stock. Other turkey calls of Grandpa's era were the homemade box calls. Cedar and walnut were two of the more favored woods. Wild turkey wing bones from a hen were also carefully crafted and used to call many a gobbler in the Ozark Mountains.

I sometimes wonder what Grandpa would think of the turkey calls of today, not only because there are so many different types, but also because they are now so much easier to use. No longer is turkey calling something that is mastered only after years of sheer repetition, whether for simple entertainment, hunting for the sport, or for feeding a growing family.

Modern technology has done a great deal to refine a practice begun hundreds of years ago by American Indians. Today's turkey hunters have it much better than hunters of even a decade ago. Nevertheless, it's tough for someone to walk into a sporting goods store, pick up any call, and be able to call in a turkey by the time he leaves. Calling still takes practice and a good knowledge of the basics. Calling takes not only practice and knowledge of the basics, it also requires knowing when, where, and how to call. My first mouth calls, known as "mouth yelpers," were homemade from plumber's lead and latex from the local Texaco station. We did not have or use tape. There were not many mouth yelpers available or many hunters using them during my early years in the Ozarks.

Today's diaphragm mouth calls are available in about one hundred different models. Frames are quality aluminum and plastics. The latex is now made from dental dam, and the thickness of the reeds varies from call to call. Single-reed, double-reed, triple-reed, split V, and Cutter four-reed are just a few designs. Many mouth calls today have multiple types of cuts in the reeds. Friction calls that were once all slate are now glass, aluminum, titanium, single, double, triple, and with a thousand types of strikers. Today's box calls come in every size and shape and are made of every available wood and plastic. Individual hunters should try numerous calls and find a particular type that works well for them, is easy to use, and that they have confidence in.

I really can't say that one particular call, or family of calls for that matter, is better than the others. Personally, I like them all. You can bet that I'll have a half dozen mouth calls, a good-quality slate call, and my old faithful box call. Each call has its place in turkey hunting. It's not unusual for me to use all three—the slate, box, and mouth calls—on the same day.

I usually tell a beginner to start with a box call; the box is the easiest to use and it sounds like a turkey. Another advantage is it is in one unit, with the lid and calling edge on the bottom part fastened together. Try other types of calls as soon as you feel comfortable with the operation and sounds of your first call.

Hunters should use a lot of common sense, practice and learn to be versatile with all kinds of calls.

The day will come when the gobbler that's ignored your diaphragm calls will all but run you over when you try a friction call. Not a season goes by that I'm not trying something new to the market. There's no doubt that being skilled with all kinds of calls, and working very hard with calls, have added to my success.

Of the two types of calls—air and friction calls—there's not much doubt that the friction is the easier to use. As the name im-

The slate call is a very realistic-sounding friction call, excellent for soft tree calls and purring. Never lift the striker from the surface when calling. Do not touch calling surfaces with your fingers.

plies, sounds are generated by rubbing two materials together. With the right materials and some practice, those calls sound like a turkey.

SLATE CALLS

Ever since my grandpa laid that first call made of broken chalkboard slate and a corncob-and-cedar striker in my hand, slate calls have always had a special place in my heart. The fact that I've used slate calls to call in hundreds of turkeys has also helped endear them to me.

Over the years I've used the soft, natural notes of slate to call in toms already down and others still on the roost. In heavy timber where the terrain allows a close setup, the soft slate is very effective.

In the late 1980s, I was hunting Merriam's late in the season in a heavily hunted area, with mixed results. I went through every type of call I had with me. On my third morning I moved in close to a roosted flock and decided to use an old slate call to send a gobbler soft tree yelps, followed by excited cutting. By the time morning fly-down arrived I had the bird in a gobbling frenzy. A friend of mine hunting with me killed the longbeard as he came running in. I found a call that sounded like a turkey, perhaps like one of his hens, a sound that particular tom responded to. Sometimes I think calling turkeys is a lot like fishing; keep throwing it out there until you find something that works.

For years the basic materials for making slate calls were similar to the homemade call that got me started. About the only variable was the handle that held the peg. Sometimes it was hollow wood and sometimes hollow corncob.

Then came Plexiglas instead of cedar in the striker, to water-proof the call and make it sound more consistent. It was a heck of an idea and it worked well.

Then a few years ago people started experimenting with new materials to replace the slate. Today you can find "slates" made of aluminum, glass, Plexiglas, acrylic, and almost any combination thereof. Slate calls can also be stacked in double and triple layers.

It seems as if every manufacturer has its own striker/slate combination of varying dimensions and materials. They all sound different.

Generally speaking, the old-fashioned wood and true slate calls sound rather mellow. They are great for soft and sweet yelps and purrs. Their only drawback, besides not being waterproof, is a lack of volume for locating gobblers or for windy days.

Some of the new materials don't seem to have the gentle finesse of the old materials. Don't get me wrong; they still sound good, but to me the soft talk isn't quite as sweet. But the upside is that the glass and acrylic calls have plenty of volume. They can make good yelps, and almost anyone can use them to imitate cutting.

It's up to the individual to choose his best slate call. If you're in the market for a good slate call I'd suggest that you look around and listen. Check with local turkey hunters to see what they favor and ask them to give you a demonstration to see how their calls sound.

Try to get your hands on as many types of slate calls as possible. You have to be physically comfortable with a call to get the most out of it. Naturally you'll want to see how easy it is to get turkey sounds from the call. The easier it is, the faster you'll learn everything, from the basics through the advanced calls.

Once you've decided on a call, the next step is to learn how to use it properly. The first and probably most important step is to start getting good, consistent sounds from the call.

If you're right-handed you should hold the slate in your left hand. Most of today's calls come with a sound chamber already built onto the bottom of the slate. If so, just hold the call as you would a can of soda pop, in close to your body.

If you have a chamberless call, it becomes important to create a good sound chamber with your hand and fingers. Again, you'll want to tuck the call in close to your body.

Hold the striker in your other hand, much as you would a pencil. Grasp the striker about an inch or two from the bottom for better control and consistency.

Place the striker near the center of the slate at a slight angle and softly draw it toward you. Go slowly at first, experimenting until you get a feel for the amount of pressure it takes to get the right notes. Once you've got the feel for the call, start moving the striker far enough to create a yelp.

Once you get a smooth, continuous sound from the call, it's time to start putting notes together. One of the biggest mistakes people make is lifting the striker from the call's surface. Keep the striker on the surface. I like to go back and forth in a straight line, but some calls sound better if you move the striker in a circular motion. Try it both ways until you find the best approach for you and your call.

Once you're able to put two notes together, try three notes, four, and so on. Strive for consistency, and remember that the turkey rhythm starts off soft and short before building to longer and louder yelps.

In my opinion the slate call produces the most realistic purrs of any call. The purr is also the easiest sound to produce. You simply draw the peg across the slate slowly, using different amounts of pressure until you achieve the sound. Chances are you were purring when you were trying to get your first sounds from the slate.

Making the cluck is just the opposite. Place the striker on the slate and snap it toward you, moving it no more than a quarter- to a half-inch. Use more pressure than you did for the purr, and don't lift the striker from the call.

Cutting on a slate is a lot easier to do than it is to explain in a book. It's actually fast and hard clucks. Once you've mastered the yelps and clucks and have heard some good cutting on a tape or from a good caller, combining the two into excited cutting will come easily.

Since you have to hold some models of slate calls close to your body, it is important for you to practice from authentic calling positions. Try sitting with your back against a tree. If you feel too cramped with the call against your abdomen, you can often move it to the inside of your leg. Once you're consistently getting good sounds from the call, practice calling with your eyes straight ahead. You do not want to be looking at the call when a big gobbler comes walking in.

As you get better, start experimenting with the hand holding the call. Even with calls that come with sound chambers, you'll be able to vary your calls by opening and closing your hand. Also, learn how to call purrs, clucks, and yelps as softly as possible.

Some hunters seem concerned that movement when using the slate will spook turkeys. Maybe, if used at the wrong time with a gobbler standing in front of you. I have never had such a problem and I have never spooked birds using a slate-type call.

The key is to keep the call low and close to your body so that your raised legs will conceal the movement. There's really less motion involved than you think; you need to move only a few fingers.

If you've chosen your calling site well, the turkey shouldn't be able to see you until he's within range. By the time the gobbler is close enough to see any call movement, you should already have the call down and the gun up and ready to go.

I like to angle the gun across my lap, the forearm resting on a raised knee and the butt on the ground. When it comes time to move for the gun, all you have to do is let the call rest on your lap and slowly move your hands to your gun. If you can see the turkey, wait to grab your gun until his head goes behind an obstruction like a tree, blowdown, or fanned tail.

Like any sound-producing instrument, slate calls require a little special care. The main objective is to protect the slate surface

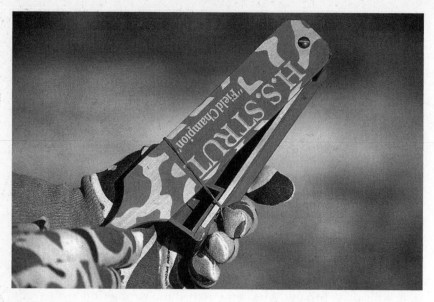

The box call is one of the most realistic-sounding turkey calls and the most easy to use.

from any material that might fill in its pores, such as dirt, dust, or even the oil from your fingertips.

To get the best sound, you'll want to keep the slate surface slightly rough with a little sandpaper or emery cloth. Don't go overboard; all it needs is an occasional brisk sanding.

How often you'll need to sand will vary from call to call. You definitely need to sand daily and every time the surface gets dirty or smoothed from being carried unprotected in a coat pocket. I also like to sand the call if it looks as if I'm going to be in one spot for a long time. The last thing you want is the sound to start to go when a gobbler is only halfway in.

When using one of the old-style, cedar-pegged calls in high humidity or even rain, carry the call in some sort of plastic bag.

BOX CALLS

Even more so than slate calls, many turkey hunters view box calls as meant only for beginners. In fact, a few years ago an outdoor writer questioned my hunting capabilities when I said I'd be using a box call. By noon that writer wanted to know where he could buy one like mine.

Box calls have as much going for them as any turkey call. They're relatively easy to use, they can get loud for locating or whisper quiet for soft talk, and they'll produce almost every call in a turkey's vocabulary.

But the most important thing is that they simply sound like turkeys. Most professional turkey hunters can easily tell the difference between a diaphragm call and a real turkey. But put someone who's good with a box call in the woods, and the pros may end up scratching their heads.

The box call can have the same effect on turkeys. Many years ago Ben Held and I headed to South Dakota's Black Hills for a shot at the Merriam's turkey.

The little set of hills that we hunted was full of signs of both turkeys and turkey hunters. We heard some distant gobbling at sunrise, but it was as if the birds had a case of lock-beak when I opened up with my diaphragm calls at fly-down time. It became very obvious that this area had intense activity from many hunters, and the turkeys were in the quiet mode.

I pulled out my weathered old box call and gave a few cuts and excited yelps. Suddenly everything changed. In scarcely more than one day and a half of hunting I called in eight different longbeards using the box call. I definitely found the sound the turkeys wanted to hear and responded well to.

That's not the first time box calls have saved me, nor will it be the last. They're simply deadly, deadly calls if you know how to use them. The principle of the box call involves drawing a wooden paddle over a rectangular wooden box. The friction created sounds like a wild turkey.

For years most box calls looked pretty much the same, the paddle hinged to a box, which was usually made of cedar or sometimes walnut. There are also smaller box calls with unattached lids on the market.

Some manufacturers have started using acrylic for call parts to prevent moisture from changing a call's tone. Since the sound is still created by wood on wood, the acrylic-containing calls are often good.

Although most box calls on the market may look alike, they sure don't sound alike. Some are good and some are not so good.

Most stores will let you take a brand out of the box and give it a few tries. If you can get away with it, try every darned call that they have. Sounds vary not only from brand to brand, but to some extent from call to call. Listen well for what sounds the best.

Move the paddle slowly across the box's edge when trying a new call. Feel whether it moves smoothly and look closely to see if it makes consistent contact with the box. If a box call can make very soft sounds it's probably tuned properly.

Once you've picked a call it's time to start some serious practice. As with the slate, start with the basics; simply get a smooth note from the call.

You'll usually want to start with the middle of the lid resting on the edge of the box, using just a little pressure to bring the lid toward the call. Try a few starting points and vary the pressure on the lid until you come up with the best sound.

If you're having problems, or even if you're not, you may want to experiment with the way you hold the call. Most hunters hold the box horizontally with the lid on top, but that might not work best for you. Some use the call horizontally with the paddle down.

For years I've had success with holding the call vertically, the hinge down. Others do well with the hinge up. Most people run the lid against the box, but there are some who hold the lid still and scrape with the box. Try all methods and decide what's best for you.

Which wall of a two-sided box you use can be another variable. Try both sides to find out which one sounds better. Some calls have sides of different thickness. The thicker of the two makes the deeper notes.

Some box calls have one side for hen notes and the other for gobbler yelps. Don't let that worry you. Either side will work for hen calls. Anyone who has listened to many turkeys has stories of hens with deep and raspy calls. If the "gobbler" side sounds best to you, use it. Neither you nor the gobblers will be disappointed.

Once you've developed your own style and consistent notes, it's time to get a little more ambitious. Go from one good note to a string of yelps. Make sure you have the ever-important turkey rhythm, and try for high and low notes in each individual sound.

Purring on a box call is as easy as drawing the lid slowly across the box. The key is to do it smoothly. Clucks are just short, snappy yelps.

Be sure to practice both ends of the volume spectrum. There will be times when the wind is howling and you'll be working the box and lid like a set of hedge clippers just to be heard.

Making the soft yelps, purrs, and clucks is probably more important. Try to get so soft that you can barely hear the sound. At that point a turkey could still probably hear the call at sixty yards. If you're having difficulty calling softly, you might stuff some tissue or a cotton glove in the chamber of the box.

Reducing movement while calling is easily accomplished. As with the slate, practice calling from a sitting position with the call between your body and your raised knees. By keeping your arms tucked into your sides, you'll need only a little hand movement.

Paying attention and having a good calling site should give you plenty of time to drop the call and lift the stock of your shotgun. Thinking back, I can't recall ever spooking a turkey just because I was using a box call.

But simply walking through the woods with the call in your

pocket can get you into trouble; the lid scrapes loudly back and forth, making a variety of obnoxious noises. Stuffing the box with a tissue or glove can help solve the problem. Using a rubber band to hold the lid down tight would be yet another solution.

Keeping a box call sounding its best is largely just a matter of keeping the calling surfaces clean of dirt, mud, oil, and other foreign substances. Another necessity is keeping the lid and edge of the box well chalked with a soft, oil-free chalk. It's best to use the specially made brown box-call chalk rather than the white and blue chalk you can buy at hardware stores. The brown chalk works best and has no oil base to it.

I like to chalk my box call first thing in the morning and again later if I'm going to be using it for any length of time. You can usually check the bottom of the lid to see when it needs a little more chalk.

Occasionally, perhaps once a year, you might want to use some light sandpaper or emery cloth to clean the lid and lip of your box call. Take your time; go gently enough that you don't scrape deep into the wood.

If you're hunting in the rain or in high humidity it's important to keep the box call as dry as possible. Carrying the call in a plastic bag between calling sites will help. If conditions get really wet, you can use the call inside the bag.

I know it sounds as if box calls can be something of a problem. But hey, you ought to look at it from the turkey's point of view.

MOUTH CALLS

Turkey hunters have been using their mouths to fool turkeys for centuries. Native Americans used just their voices, or sucked on an old turkey wing bone to call birds.

I've used pipe stems, soda straws, and ink pens to call gobblers. A good friend, Damon Jarvis, could put most calls and callers to shame with a wild cherry leaf.

But mouth calls, commonly known as diaphragm calls, are without a doubt the most popular calls in the turkey woods today. Some hunters like them because they leave both hands free for handling the gun. Others choose them because they're compact. The pure challenge of mastering the call is yet another reason for the diaphragm call's popularity.

There are several theories about the origin of diaphragm calls, but I guess the theories aren't as important as how the calls work. Most mouth calls consist of a piece of latex stretched tight between a folded aluminum horseshoe that's covered with a piece of tape. Air blown over the call causes the latex to vibrate rapidly, and those vibrations can be transformed into turkey calls.

Sounds simple, doesn't it? Those who have been around the calls for a couple of decades will tell you that it's not nearly as simple as it used to be.

Originally all diaphragm calls consisted of a single reed. I can remember making my own single-reed calls by cutting up condoms and stretching the latex between plumber's lead in the late 1960s. Even back then I didn't think much of the single-reed calls. The calls worked, but to me they never quite sounded like real turkeys.

Later someone tried using two pieces of latex, one stretched slightly behind the other. That development got me much more interested in diaphragm calls, and I spent more and more time cutting condoms and lead. Multiple-reed mouth calls could be made to sound like turkeys and weren't too hard to use. Things really snowballed from there.

Obviously the next step up in complexity was the triple-reed call. When necessary it produces more volume, but is still capable of good soft talk in the mouth of a skilled caller. I've always considered it a call for the intermediate to advanced caller.

There are also mouth calls with four—or even more—reeds on

the market, but I really question whether they have many advantages for most turkey hunters. To be honest, I rarely use them myself.

Then hunters started discovering the advantages of split reeds. I'm talking about calls with either slits or even large holes in the longest, uppermost reed.

The first time I heard such a call was quite by accident years ago. Mike Held and I were hunting when Mike stopped and tried to separate the reeds on his call with his fingers. As luck (and I do mean luck) would have it, one of the reeds tore. Mike cussed a little but threw the call in anyway. Both of our eyes lit up like neon signs when we heard his new call. Suddenly I started ripping many of my favorite calls.

The rips make the latex vibrate even more, giving the call every bit as much rasp as a cranked-up hen turkey. The larger the slit or tear, the raspier the call. It's a sound that's popular with turkeys and turkey hunters alike.

There are basically two kinds of slits in diaphragm calls. One is actually a pair of tiny slits, one on each edge of the call. These calls are usually double reeds; they're easy to use, yet have a raspy tone.

The other kind is made by removing a chunk of latex about as big as a pencil eraser from the upper reed. The most common calls were originally triple or quadruple reeds, known as 2.5 and 3.5, respectively. They offer more than enough rasp but can be a little tough for some people to blow.

Just when the cut calls started becoming popular, yet another style of diaphragm call was introduced. Some callers are getting good sounds from these calls, which put each reed within its own frame. (The original calls stretched the reeds across one single frame.) Such calls can make some good sounds but may feel a little awkward and chunky in the mouths of many hunters.

Combine all of the possibilities of multiple- and cut-reed calls with the two sizes that most major call manufacturers produce and you have quite a selection of calls out there. In fact, there are so many that it's starting to get confusing for beginning and intermediate callers.

The double-reed call is still, and probably always will be, the best all-around call on the market. It is absolutely the easiest to learn on and is easily blown, and it can produce a wide range of turkey sounds for most hunters.

I suggest that most beginners get started with a double-reed call. Once they feel comfortable with it they can move to a double-reed that has a pair of tiny slits, which is still easy to handle yet sounds realistic.

Probably the next step would be a 2.5. It can take a little getting used to, but once a hunter has it down there's not a call he can't make in the woods.

The level of skill a hunter reaches is just a matter of personal preference. I know many excellent callers who stick with the double, raspy double, and the 2.5 for all of their calling.

This may sound strange if you haven't tried it, but possibly the hardest part of learning to use a diaphragm call is simply being able to tolerate the call resting on the roof of the mouth. The body naturally doesn't want to tolerate something that large near the throat; many people gag.

Everyone has to break himself in at his own pace. I believe that too many people expect things to happen too quickly. For most people, learning to use a mouth call isn't something to start a week or two before the season.

It's best to begin by simply holding the call between your lips for a while. Next, move the call inward so that it's between your teeth and cheek at the side of your mouth.

If that's no problem, then try to put the call on the roof of your mouth, the open end facing out and the call far enough forward that the front of the frame rests against the back of your gums. Be sure that the longest reed is at the top. Hold it in place for a few seconds if you can. Then remove your fingers and try shutting your mouth as you hold the call in place with the middle of your tongue.

If the call simply won't fit (the frame is too big), you may want to try a smaller call. If the frame will fit but the call still feels too big, then you may want to take some scissors and start trimming the tape from around the call. Take it easy when you cut; remove only a hair at a time until the call will fit in place.

There are some people who have no problems tolerating the call in their mouths. I've seen a person slip a call into his mouth for the first time without any negative reaction. Some people need months to get used to the feel, and others gag every time.

Hunters who simply can't handle a diaphragm needn't worry. The friction, slate, and box calls can be just as effective and are actually easier to use. Someone who wants the sound of a mouth call can switch to a tube call, which is actually the same latex stretched over a plastic tube. The call rests on the outside of your mouth, so wouldn't cause any gagging.

Once you can hold a diaphragm inside your mouth, it's time to start working on making some sort of noise. First, make sure the call is properly fitted against the roof of your mouth and is held lightly in place by the front part of your tongue.

Next, try to force a steady stream of air from your gut over the call. It's not like whistling, but more like saying a long, drawn-out word like "chuck." Don't worry about what sounds you get. The important thing is that you get some sound from the call.

Practice until you can get a steady, unwavering note for a few seconds. Don't get discouraged if it takes some time. It will come. When you can, start using a little tongue pressure to get the high part of a yelp. After that's become easy, back your tongue off a little and the tone will change to the low part at the end of the yelp.

From there on you gradually shorten the sounds, making sure that you have the high and low on each call. It may help to keep repeating "chuck." The next thing you know you're yelping.

No matter what your spouse or friends say, there's no such thing as too much practice. Beginners ought to have the call in their mouths every day. Call while riding to and from work and any other times you can get away with it. You need to be able to call without really concentrating.

If you have a friend who's a good caller, try to mimic him. Invest in a good instructional tape and call along with it. Practice, practice, practice.

Once you've gotten some control over the call, start working on calling very softly as well as quickly and slowly. Practice making a single yelp and a string of up to thirty yelps.

After you've mastered the simple yelp, try getting some short clucks from the call. Simply popping your lips together can usually make the sounds of such short-note calls as putts.

Purring is a little more difficult, both to explain and to accomplish.

Try to loosen your tongue on your call so that your tongue vibrates when you blow air through your mouth. Stick with it. It's the kind of thing that might elude you for weeks or months and then suddenly it will just start to work for you.

Taking a tape recorder to the woods is an excellent way to see how you sound. Tape your calls on the recorder; then back off about sixty yards to see how you'll sound to the turkeys.

Many hunters put their hands to their mouths for simple comfort while others do so to improve their sound. Putting a cupped hand to your mouth does more than just improve sound. I use my hand like a small megaphone to send calls in different directions. Most turkeys don't stand in one spot to do all their calling, so I try to sound like a bird that's walking around.

Experienced and novice hunters alike need to remember that there's no such thing as being too good with a diaphragm call. Keep practicing and don't be afraid to try something different. Once you've mastered one call, try a more difficult one. Check the market from time to time and look for innovations.

Do some experimenting with a couple of new calls every year, and don't rule out trying different manufacturers. You never know when there might be something better out there.

Spend as much time as possible listening to good turkey calling from tapes, CDs, videos, and at turkey calling contests. Ask someone for help if there's a call you're having problems with. There may be a shortcut that could work well for you.

Like all instruments, diaphragm turkey calls require a little care to work their best. Keep the calls in their protective cases when they're not in your mouth, and never leave them near intense heat or in direct sunlight.

There are a wide variety of diaphragm mouth calls to choose from. Experiment until you find the design that works best for you. Mouth calls reproduce a wide range of turkey talk.

If your call is dry and your reeds are stuck together, don't start pulling and jerking. The reeds rip easily. Instead, wallow the call around in your mouth for a while and let it get good and wet. Calling may vibrate the reeds open. If it doesn't, try holding the call between your fingers and softly blowing some air to free the reeds.

Diaphragm calls will last longer if stored in a refrigerator or freezer when they're not in use. Carefully sliding flat toothpicks between the reeds is another little trick that can help extend the life of a call.

VOICE

One advantage to calling with your vocal cords is that they're always with you. Your voice can also sound more natural than an artificial call. There are times when a turkey will readily respond to the natural sounds of a good voice caller.

Looking back over the years, I've called more turkeys with my voice than any other way, and I've taught a lot of hunters how use voice calls regularly. With practice, most turkey hunters can master them.

As with all calls, the voice call is tough to explain on paper. Mouth yelping basically revolves around the word "calk." Start off saying the word regularly, then begin taking it up in pitch, gradually moving it to the back of your throat.

Don't force it. Having your throat and vocal cords relaxed is important. Give yourself plenty of time and stick with it. There's probably no bigger thrill in calling than using your natural voice to harvest a wild turkey.

Turkey hunters trying to take advantage of a spring tom's excited gobbling have several locating calls to choose from. Most are inexpensive and easy to use.

OWL HOOTER

Even a small child can get owl hoots from one of the small, barrel-shaped owl hooters that are currently on the market. Many avid hunters take the time to learn how to make the notes of a barred owl using only their voices. It can be a lot of fun and very effective once you get the hang of it.

CROW CALL

The crow call is probably the most universal of all locating calls. Coast to coast, turkeys readily respond to the shrill caws of a number of manufactured crow calls. The higher the pitch the better; keep the calls short and excited.

OTHER CALLS

Hunters can also utilize the high squeal of hawk and predator calls, coyote howlers, and elk bugles. A tight, triple-reed call can be used to make the high-pitched screams of the same calls.

6

YEAR-ROUND SCOUTING

Over the years many people have asked me when they should begin scouting for turkey season. A good turkey hunter actually scouts year-round.

I spend much of my summer, fall, and winter looking over new turkey country. I'm not looking for turkeys as much as I am good habitat. Experience will tell you what the turkeys in your home state prefer.

Look for a good stand of timber. Obviously that varies from region to region. For the Rio Grande hunter it may be as skimpy as a few cottonwoods along a dry creek or a long, towering evergreen shelterbelt. Such surroundings would rarely deserve a second look in good eastern country.

No matter where they're from, a few good turkey hunters always seem to tag a bird on opening morning. Over the years I've met many of these hunters, and they're all different. Some carry a wide selection of new mouth calls, and some use a weathered old box call that's fooled hundreds of turkeys through many generations. But there is one thing each of these never-fail hunters has in common—scouting. They know exactly where the turkeys are at any given time of any given day. That makes things much easier. No matter how good you are, you can't call very many turkeys if there aren't any there.

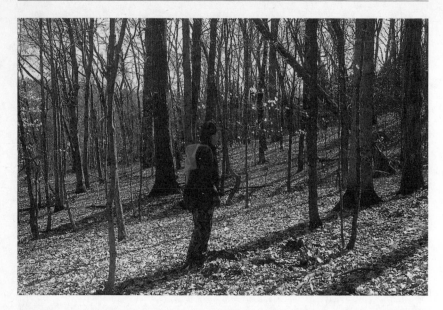

Scouting your hunting area before spring green-up gives you the opportunity to learn the lay of the land. This hunter is looking for fresh turkey signs such as tracks, feathers, poop, and scratchings.

Finding water is another of the most important considerations when scouting a new area.

Good turkey habitat also needs adequate food and water. If you're planning to hunt the spring season you should look for plenty of good nesting habitat. Find a place with nesting hens in the spring and you'll find gobblers.

If you're new to the area, or if your state's still in a restocking program, you may want to make sure there are birds around before spending much time scouting. Local landowners and conservation agents are good sources of information, as are rural mail carriers and school bus drivers.

A lot of hunters, myself included, like to combine turkey scouting trips with fall hunting. The thousands of hours I've spent combing the woods for squirrels and whitetails have been a big help during turkey seasons.

The fall and winter is an excellent time to get to know the lay of the land. Look for barriers like creeks, fences, and steep bluffs. Find where game and logging trails begin and end.

Look for potential strutting areas and calling sites. It's a lot easier to get a feel for the land when the leaves are on the ground.

Learn the different ways you can approach an area. Finding the back door into a good piece of public property can give you a big advantage over the competition.

Of course you want to keep an eye out for the turkeys themselves, but don't be overly concerned if you don't see any on your winter scouting trips. In many regions turkeys travel to wintering areas, where they may build flocks of several hundred birds.

Where these wintering birds congregate is usually common knowledge. You can ask conservation agents or local landowners if you don't already know. If possible, check in on the flock from time to time so you'll know when the birds begin to disperse in the spring.

In the meantime, get to know the property. The more time you can spend looking over the lay of the land when the season is still months away, the better. You'll want to devote the few weeks before opening day concentrating on finding and learning about individual birds.

When it looks as if spring is here to stay, it's time to start walking, looking, and listening. Look for tracks around the edges of fields, at creek crossings, along dirt roads—any place they might show in the soil. Naturally, gobbler tracks are going to be noticeably larger than hen tracks. But generally, where you find hens, you'll find gobblers when the mating season rolls around.

Droppings are another good indicator of an area's turkey population. Most people already know how to distinguish the J-shaped gobbler droppings from the round, popcorn-like ones of a hen. Keep your eyes open for feathers, scratchings, and dusting areas as well.

Hunters also need to realize that where they live determines what they're looking for when scouting. There are places in good Rio Grande habitat where you can walk all day and not see any scratch-

The larger the track the larger the turkey. Gobbler tracks are anywhere from 3½ to 4½ inches from heel to toe.

Good turkey sign is fresh tracks that are clearly visible in soft dirt or sand. Old trails, field edges, and creek banks are good places to look for tracks.

ings. But if you look closely, you might notice that most of the cow pies have been overturned—by turkeys pecking the bugs and worms from beneath. I've seen the same thing in eastern habitat as well.

Relying strictly on droppings can be misleading when hunting mountain Merriam's. Due to low humidity and the makeup of their diet, what the turkeys pass may not disintegrate for days.

Your ears can help you cover a lot of ground even if the toms aren't gobbling much. A few good fall calls can often get an old hen or gobbler yelping. You can also listen for wingbeats and roost talk at first and last light.

In some areas a good pair of binoculars can help you find the birds. From a high point, check fields and meadows for birds feeding or sunning in the early morning or late afternoon.

When the toms start gobbling, your scouting gets a whole lot easier, but it's as important as ever. I try to spend many mornings cruising the edges of my hunting grounds, listening for gobbles.

Some of the freshest sign of all—moist droppings. Hunters can tell a lot from droppings: the size of the bird, its gender, and what it has been feeding on.

Another good sign that a gobbler is in the area is a fresh black-tipped feather.

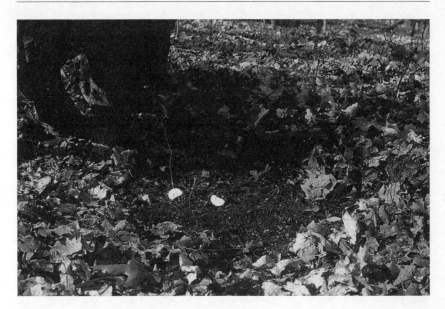

Wild turkeys scratch through the leaves on the forest floor looking for food.

Sighting birds in the area you plan to hunt is the best turkey sign of all.

If you know an area well and hunt it often, sometimes you won't need to start scouting until the birds are gobbling. In good, unchanged habitat gobblers stay in the same general places from one season to the next.

Depending on where the birds are in their breeding cycle, you may be able to get responses to a locating call. It's also fairly safe to use a gobble now. Try to check as many spots as possible during that half hour when birds are gobbling from the roost.

One of the biggest mistakes you can make is to pressure the turkeys with human activity; the birds change patterns. But with a little caution, scouting from a distance, listening to the gobblers, you can learn so much just a few days before the season.

Despite what some people say, I do quite a bit of calling a few weeks before the season. Some say it educates the birds. I say it educates the hunter, provided he doesn't overdo it by calling the bird in close and spooking it.

I can't count the times I've called to a certain bird every day for a week before the season. I'm not talking about pouring it on; I'd call just enough to get him to sound off once. But on opening morning I'd know right where he'd be. I would move in close and pour it on, and he'd run right to me.

If possible, I use a locating call at first light and move in close while the birds are still on the roost so that I can learn where they head when they fly down. No matter how well I know an area, I also take the time to check it one last time, looking for any changes.

A couple of days before the season is the time to check the meadows and clearings for strutting turkeys, breast feathers, or the marks made by dragging wingtips to see if an area is used for strutting. If you're lucky you'll find indications that a bird uses a spot day after day.

If you've done your job, you should know the general location of anywhere from six to sixty gobblers before the season opens.

Strive to remember everything you've learned about each one of them.

Personally, I always carry a topographic map to chart the location of each gobbler I hear, making special note of high densities or a bird with easily discernible behavior patterns. If you make such a map, keep it hidden and guard it with your life. You may be able to trust your best friend or brother with your car, children, or deepest secret—but not with a piece of paper that shows the way to a quartet of toms that are gobbling their brains out all morning. (You could, of course, trust me.)

Remember that you never really stop scouting, not even when the season begins. Keep your eyes open as you move through the woods. Things can change for better or worse from day to day.

Hunters who find themselves hunting unfamiliar territory can scout as they go. Cover as much ground as possible so you can learn

Look for dusting bowls when scouting.

the lay of the land and the ways of the turkeys. If you hear some gobbling or find some fresh sign, stop and work the area.

Keep your ears and eyes open for other hunters. Drive the roads in your hunting area and look for parked vehicles as you enter and leave to see if you have company. If so, you may want to either approach from another direction or perhaps even try another site.

Thanks to your good scouting, you'll know right where to go.

7

BASICS FOR HUNTING THE MATING SEASON

It's almost magical, this time of indecision between night and day. The woods at your destination may be rolling seas of hardwoods or thin ribbons of cottonwoods. Either way, they are full of invitation as you enter in the predawn grayness. Even in the gloom your eyes pick up the ivory blossoms of a budding dogwood or sand plum; your nostrils become alive with their sweet fragrance. The dew-laden grasses feel cool and wet as they brush against your legs.

But it's your ears and what they hear that demand your full attention. As the increasing light spreads across the eastern horizon, so do the sounds of the new day. First comes the occasional chirp of a songbird or maybe the raspy call of a cock pheasant.

By the time you reach your stopping place the woods are in full chorus. Songbirds flit about while the mournful sounds of a great horned owl roll across the land.

Yet you wait for the one sound that has been on your mind for months—the rattling gobble of a turkey. You needn't look at your watch to know it could erupt at any second. The brightening woods and your quickening pulse tell you it's gobbling time.

It is without a doubt the most exciting time of the day. It's also the time of the most uncertainty. Will there be any gobbling to be heard? Where will it come from? Will you be able to get there in time to work the bird while he's still on the limb?

You can rest a little more comfortably if you've scouted before the season. Success is almost a sure thing if you scouted the woods the night before.

8

ROOSTING BIRDS

Dusk was still more than an hour away as I made my way across a long Ozark ridge that was intersected by a series of smaller adjoining ridges. It was the day before the Missouri opener, and I was on this ridge by choice. My preseason scouting had revealed that there were several toms in the area. One big old bird was the unmistakable boss.

Roosting, or as some call it "putting a bird to bed," is basically waiting in the woods at dusk and listening for a gobbler to betray his location. Once he's discovered, you know exactly where to begin the next morning's hunt. If all goes well you can sneak in close and work the gobbler on the roost when he's probably the most vulnerable to calling.

In the right situation, roosting can be a very effective tactic.

Moving as quietly as possible, I sat down in a place where I could hear down several of the small ridges, and waited. The shadows of sunset extended almost from horizon to horizon when the bird's first gobble split the silence.

Many hunters would have been content just to know the bird's general location, but the more precisely you can pinpoint a bird the better. He sounded about three hundred yards away. I started a slow, quiet stalk toward his roost, stopping occasionally to give a soft great horned owl hoot to get him to gobble.

I stopped about eighty yards short of the bird, taking a seat beside an old oak that was at about the same level as the gobbler and near the edge of an old logging road. Egged on by my hoots and the natural sounds of the forest, the old bird was still hammering out gobbles when I crept from the moonlit hillside.

It was hard not to be confident. I can't prove the theory, but it seems as if birds that are fired up in the evening are usually in the same frame of mind the next morning.

With my strategy already planned, I quietly sneaked back to the old oak long before daylight. With the first signs of light and sounds of songbirds, I gave a few soft tree yelps. There was no gobble, but the sound of the tom drumming on a limb told me we were still in business.

A little later I hit him with a few yelps. He answered with a long chorus of gobbles. He gobbled at almost everything: other turkeys gobbling in the distance, crows, owls, and sometimes at nothing at all.

With fly-down time at hand, I was afraid his nonstop gobbling might attract some camouflaged attention. So I opened up with a series of fast cackles like a hen flying down from a limb. After pausing a few seconds I came back with some soft, soothing purrs—like a hen content to move around on the ground.

The big tom flew down and triple-gobbled on the old logging road about fifty yards to my right. Again, I sent him some aggressive cutting, which brought him in at a fast trot, slowing only to gobble and break into a half-strut. I was back in camp by 6 A.M.

The tom was large for a mountain bird, 23½ pounds, with an 11½-inch beard and, even more impressively, 1½-inch spurs.

It's too bad all roosting episodes don't end with such ease and happiness. Roosting turkeys vary a lot. For one thing, the birds have to be in good gobbling cycles. Hit them too early or too late in the breeding season and there will be little, if any, limb talk.

There can also be a great deal of variety across the country. In my home state of Missouri it's getting tougher to get even a single evening gobble, but I've had as many as eight or ten different Merriam's responding well to calls long after dark in South Dakota's Black Hills.

I think that hunting pressure has more to do with it than breeding. Throughout the early 1970s, I can remember being in the only camp in a section of national forest in Missouri, listening to turkeys gobbling all around us as we ate supper. That same ground now has about as many hunters as trees, and it's tough to get a bird to gobble in the morning, let alone the evening.

But if you have the time, and the birds are right, roosting can definitely be worth the effort. Try and get into the woods an hour before dark. Go where you know there are turkeys, but try to get away from the commotion of roads or running water. If possible, stick to the high country where you can hear more territory.

One of the main objectives is not to disturb the surroundings and the turkeys. Spend more time listening than calling, and keep your ears open for hen talk, gobbling, and the wingbeats of birds flying up to roost.

Most hunters wisely opt for natural locating calls, such as owl hoots, crow calls, or coyote howls. Try to use what the birds might have been gobbling at for days. If you're hunting eastern turkeys, that might be barred owl hoots. If Rios are your birds, try crow or coyote calls.

And don't limit yourself to one call. Just because they aren't gobbling at one doesn't mean that they won't go nuts over another. I once used a shrill crow call and got but a single Merriam's gobble,

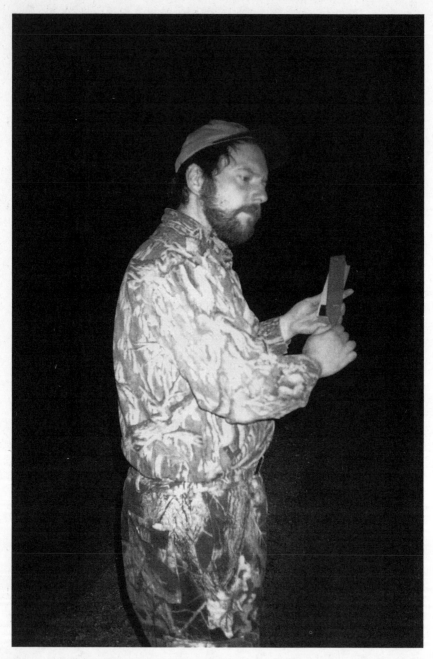

The most popular locating or "roosting" call is the owl hooter. However, cutting and yelping on a box call right at dark works best of all.

but seconds later a high-pitched coyote howl from a diaphragm call brought seven different responses. The next night the gobblers' reactions could have been just the opposite. Don't try to figure them out; just be prepared to try anything.

And that anything should include hen calls. Sure, you don't hear much about them, but that doesn't mean they won't work. For one thing, soft talk may get a response from some otherwise silent hens.

There are also times during the breeding season when gobblers don't seem to gobble at anything but hen calls. The first time I hunted Massachusetts with Gerry Bethge, Editor-in-Chief of Harris Publications, I could crow or owl until my lungs ached and not get a gobble. When I opened up with some aggressive hen calls on a box call, though, I couldn't get the turkeys to shut up.

As with any calling, hen calls should start off softly with a few clucks and yelps, gradually building in volume and intensity to excited cutting and cackling at fly-up time.

There are several theories on the best way to venture into the woods at roosting time. Most hunters like to separate and spread out to cover as much ground as possible. If one hunter hears several different birds, everybody in camp might have a gobbler to work at dawn.

But John Hauer likes to use the buddy system when guiding hunters in the Black Hills. Hauer, who can move faster than a white-tailed deer through rock and pine country, likes his hunters in one spot blowing a locating call to keep a bird gobbling while he sneaks in close. Come morning, he often knows the exact tree in which the turkey sits, and his calling site is already chosen and free of debris. That bird usually doesn't live to gobble from another roost.

But there are several other items to keep in mind when it comes to roosting turkeys. One is other hunters. Get a gobbler to respond eight or ten times in an evening on crowded public ground, and the closest road may look like a used-car lot the next morning.

Roosting is not always a sure thing, but knowing the exact location of a turkey is good for your confidence. This gobbler flew down and came in early, even before all his hens were off the roost.

Additionally, the evening's events may have nothing to do with those of the morning. You can go into an area in the evening and hear nothing, but at dawn you'll hear four or five gobblers.

On a positive side, it's often the most dominant birds that do the roost gobbling. Finding a good gobbling bird in the evening may mean working a bird with golf tee-sized spurs the next morning.

And not everyone has the time or desire to go out and roost birds.

Personally, I seldom roost birds on my home hunting grounds in Missouri for the simple reason that my scouting has already shown me where the birds are.

Granted, hearing a bird sound off from his perch is a big help, but if you don't, that doesn't mean you're out of luck come morning. No, if you play your cards right you can still have a heck of a duel on your hands with the coming of dawn.

9

FIRST-LIGHT TACTICS

During the spring gobbler season there is no time more exciting or awaited with more anticipation than those magical minutes right as turkeys are awakening on the roost to a new dawn.

Consequently, it's far better to be a little early than a little late. I like to be at my listening post at least twenty minutes before gobbling time. Of course it's best to be in the place your scouting has shown to be populated with the most birds, or in an area with several birds and without other hunters.

Sometimes I think about just sleeping in, getting some much-needed rest, and hunting the turkeys after fly-down, but the attraction of that early morning hour is much too strong. Some days you can hear more gobbling in these twenty minutes than in the next ten hours. This is also the time when your chances for success are the best, especially when the hunting is tough. You don't want to miss even a minute of it.

When hunting in rolling country, try to stick to high ground, such as a main ridge. That way you can hear well, and you're also in a central location to move toward gobbling birds. You can also cover more ground more quickly if one area proves disappointing.

If the birds are gobbling well you won't need to worry about a locating call. But if it's getting light and the other birds are in full

Stick to the high country until a bird responds. This principle is the same nationwide.

voice, you may want to try an owl hoot or crow calls. If they don't work, then try some hen talk.

Again, start off softly. Every day of the season some hunter gives a hoot at the top of his lungs and scares a tom that was just waking up a short distance down the ridge.

Also, don't make your locating calls too complex. If a bird is really fired up, he may answer so quickly that your own noise keeps you from hearing him. Get loud and aggressive only when the soft and short calls aren't working.

If fly-down time is rapidly approaching and you still haven't heard a bird, you may want to consider moving on to a different area. Just because the birds aren't gobbling doesn't mean they aren't there, but in most cases the more a bird gobbles on the roost the more apt he is to respond to your calls when he's on the ground. If you have only this place to hunt, set up where birds have gobbled in the past. If you still get no response, move and call your entire hunting area.

But let's say that everything goes well instead. You get to your chosen spot, light is just beginning to spread through the trees, and it happens—a bird gobbles. Seconds later you hoot and he double-gobbles a reply. What you do next depends a lot on how far away the bird is and what the gobbling has been like on past mornings.

If you've been on this same ridge for three days straight and he's the first bird you've heard, then you probably shouldn't waste any time getting to him. But, if you know there are many birds in the area and that first gobble comes from way off, you may want to wait a few minutes to see what happens.

It's tough to hold back, but a little patience may well be rewarded. As sure as you make a beeline for that first gobble in the predawn, you'll walk right out and spook a bird that was even closer. You'll probably do this at least once in your turkey hunting career. And when you do, you'll feel just as stupid as I do when I spook a bird that was only one hundred yards away to chase one that was five times as far off.

You also don't want to rush off without some kind of game plan in mind. Spend a few moments trying to picture the terrain near the bird's location. If you don't know exactly where the bird is, look for barriers like swamps and rivers while you're still in a position to avoid them.

Unless the bird is really close you'll want to move closer. How close? It's a question of feet, but I like to get absolutely as close as possible. The farther you have to call a bird, the more that can go wrong. The longer he's on the ground, the greater the chance a real hen will make an interception.

The same thing goes for other hunters, both two- and four-legged. On a past Rio Grande hunt I had a heck of a problem with coyotes setting up between me and the birds I was working. I practically had to set up in a turkey's lap to get him in before the coyotes came.

One of the biggest and most frequent mistakes hunters make is heading directly at a gobbling bird. It's the shortest route but it's also a good way to spook a turkey.

I like to circle around before coming in on a gobbling bird, for a number of reasons. One is that you can never be totally sure how close a gobbler is. He may sound three hundred yards away simply because he's gobbling in a hollow or facing away from you on the roost. If so, you could easily stumble upon him when you think you have room to spare.

Another problem can occur when you use hen calls: The bird can fly down and head right toward you.

But you can still be in good shape if your approach cuts an arch. Even if you've overrun the bird's roost, all you have to do is circle back and you're in business.

Another often overlooked mistake when moving and setting up on a turkey is getting sky-lighted along a hill or ridge top. It may seem dark, but there will almost always be enough light for a gobbler to see you against the sky. Try to keep a ridge between you and the gobbler's location.

There's no way I can tell you exactly how close to get. I've actually moved in as close as forty yards, but other times open woods have forced me to stay as far as two hundred yards back. It all depends on the terrain and your chances of slipping in without spooking the bird. If you're the kind of hunter who makes a lot of noise when he's walking, then just accept that fact and hang a little farther back. The same rule holds if the woods are as open as a city park.

But ideally, I like to set up within seventy-five to one hundred yards of a roosted bird. It's just as important, though, to be on the right side of the bird.

Whenever I'm moving toward a bird on the roost I try to figure out in which direction he would naturally head. Sometimes it's a simple process of elimination; the birds won't usually fly down into thick brush or onto really steep hillsides.

Ideally, it's best to be set up on the same level as the gobbler, or maybe a little higher. Try to pick a route that will make it easy for the bird to get to you—no fences, thick brambles, or standing water. If you can set up along a natural travel lane like an old logging road or game trail, so much the better.

Sometimes, if you pay attention, the turkeys can let you know the best side to set up for a roosted gobbler. If you hear the tom answering the calls of hens or other toms farther away, it might be best to set up between the two groups.

Also think back to how the birds have been reacting over the past few days. Awareness of even a vague pattern can work to your benefit.

In 1987, *Fishing & Hunting Journal* editor Ron Kruger and I were in southern Kansas for the opening day of the first season that allowed nonresident turkey hunters. A friend had gotten us permission to hunt near an abandoned farm. He claimed that the birds usually roosted north of the old home, then fed in the nearby area.

We sounded a crow call near the old place, and a bird immediately answered. But he and the rest of a flock were roosting in some trees several hundred yards south of the house, not north as our friend had claimed. Figuring the birds would want to stay in the same area to feed, we set up between the house and the birds.

We were right. One particular gobbler was cutting all of my calls and came strutting to within twenty steps—where Ron took him the minute the season opened. Had we set up on one of the other sides of the house, the bird may not have come in or may have come a little more slowly. I'll never know, because given a choice I'll call from the place where the bird already wants to go.

10

EARLY TO MIDMORNING TACTICS

It happens to all hunters at some point in time during the spring turkey hunt: At first light the area you hunt is dreadfully silent. Or maybe you just did not locate or set up on a gobbling bird. If you did locate a bird, maybe you spent way too much time on a turkey that's gobbled to you from the roost, but refuses to come in.

It's possible that the bird you're working at daylight simply quits gobbling after fly-down, for whatever reason. For me this means it's probably time to find a bird that's still talking. Yes, there are times when the classic hunt of working a bird on a limb doesn't unfold as it should. It's disappointing, but it's far from the end of the hunt. It simply means you must find a bird with both feet on the ground that is willing to use them to come to you. Just because one bird will not cooperate, this doesn't mean that you can't find another that will charge right in to your gun.

Spend a few seconds recalling where you've heard other gobblers that morning, or on previous hunts within the immediate area. If there isn't any gobbling, it may be time to change to a new area, giving the birds in your present area some much-needed rest. I stick to the high country when moving and calling to locate a bird on the ground. I use the same locating calls that I use in the morning or evening—especially the owl hoots and crow calls.

If the birds have been gobbling well at all, I try to cover a lot of ground. How far I travel between calling sites depends on the weather, and my confidence in the immediate area. In Missouri, I usually go only about two hundred yards before giving the birds another call. If it's windy I may cut the distance in half, but if it's dead calm and I'm on a really high ridge I may double it.

When using locating calls, you don't really have to spend a lot of time in one place. If a gobbler is going to respond to a hoot or crow call, he'll usually do it after a series or two.

But sometimes the birds don't respond to locating calls. How they react on and off the roost tells you whether you'll need to use turkey calls for locating gobblers. Generally, if there's little limb talk,

If you do not have success early, move quietly through your area and call until you strike a bird. This gobbler was taken at midmorning in the Missouri Ozarks.

you can hang up the hoots and crow calls. It's time to talk one-on-one.

But first you should realize the problems of using turkey talk when you're moving and calling. One is that the bird may run right in before you get a chance to set up. The second is the element of danger. No matter how much hunters preach safety and positive identification, there are still people out there who stalk turkey calls and shoot at sounds and/or movement.

It usually pays to do a quick setup when you're moving and hen calling. After you've let the woods settle a little, make a few soft yelps or clucks to break the ice. If nothing gobbles, start building both intensity and volume.

Don't make the mistake of using only one or two standard calls. If the birds are really quiet it may take some excitement or a loud and high-pitched box call to get them going.

And this is a prime case where good calling—like really excited cutting and gobbler yelps—can make the difference between success and failure. During the 1988 spring season in Missouri (and in most states hunted that year), long and lively cutting was the only call the birds responded to consistently.

But no matter what the reason, suppose you just got a bird to gobble at one of your calls. Now what? Do you hold your ground, back up, move forward, lie down, stand up . . . ?

Again, each situation is unique. You have to evaluate the terrain between you and the bird: how far he is, where he is, where he's going, what's between you and him, and whether he gets to you easily and quickly.

If the responding gobbler sounds as if he's so close he's within gun range—and on rare occasions this happens—I hold my ground and don't move a muscle.

If he sounds as if he's within one hundred yards I may try to bring him on in. But otherwise I seldom try to work a bird without getting closer to him. Working a bird long distance is only asking for trouble in the form of hens, other hunters, or any number of inter-ruptions. The shorter the distance, the fewer the possible problems.

Additionally, moving toward the bird, even by only thirty or forty yards, adds a great deal of realism to your calling. You sound like a hen that's really looking for a gobbler. If he thinks you're moving in his general direction he may get excited enough to come meet you.

As with a bird on the roost, gobbling turkeys should never be approached head on. Try to figure out the path the bird will prob-ably take as he's moving in your direction. If you're on one ridge and he gobbles from another, you may want to hustle over and set up in the saddle where the two ridges meet.

On the other hand, if you're on a fairly steep ridge and the bird gobbles from a meadow below, you may have to cut around and work him from the same level. Whatever you do, make it as easy as possible for the bird to come to you.

Don't waste a lot of time, but don't be in a big hurry either. Your next move—choosing a good calling position—is one of the most important. It's also the key mistake many hunters make.

11

SETTING UP

The biggest mistake, without a doubt, is where and how a turkey hunter sets up on a bird. A successful setup also depends on the type of terrain you're hunting, be it timber, open fields, mountains, or the prairies of the West. You should try to find a calling position that will work in that given area, in that situation, that time of year, and in relation to the species of turkey you're hunting.

The setup, or calling position, in my opinion is one of the most important elements in successfully calling and killing turkeys. Where do you set up? How far from the gobbling turkey? How do you set up? So many questions, so little time. You've chosen what you feel is the easiest, most natural route for him to take. Sure, it's tempting to set up where you can watch the bird coming for a long way. But remember that the more you can see of a gobbler the better his chances of either seeing you or figuring out that something isn't right. In timber or heavily wooded mountains, whenever possible, I like to set up so that I can't see the gobbler (and vice versa) until he's within killing range. I've always liked a little break in the hill between us—or maybe a sharp bend in a treeline or logging road.

It's best if the vegetation is thick enough to block the bird's view but not his progress. You want the turkey to be able to move

Always try to set up against a tree wider than your shoulders, out of any direct sunlight. Follow the movement of the approaching turkey by sound and keep your head up off the gun until it's time to shoot.

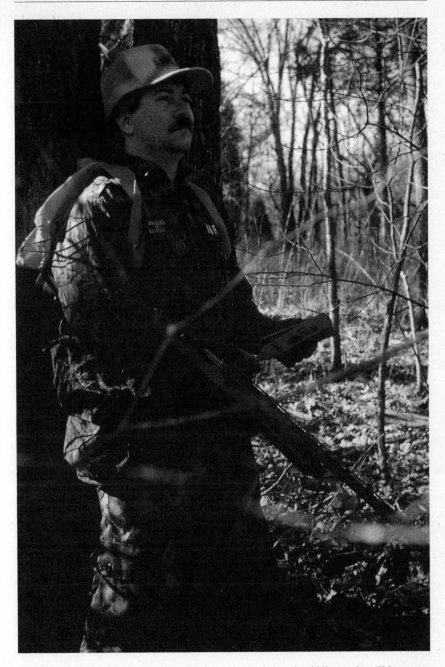

Stop in the shadows and call when moving toward a located gobbling turkey. This creates the illusion of a hen going to the gobbler. Wear hunter orange when moving and calling through the woods.

without the fear of being ambushed by predators, yet blinded enough that he's lured on by the hen that is just out of sight.

Most of the time calling from a sitting position is best. It puts you at about eye level with the turkey and usually offers a reasonable field of view.

Try to find a tree that's at least as wide as your shoulders to shield your outline. Take a few seconds to clear away anything that might interfere with your gun movement or become uncomfortable to sit on for any amount of time.

Remember that you don't have to tunnel into the ground or shield yourself with a lot of cover. One of my biggest, and now funniest, mistakes was trying to set up inside a dense bunch of brambles when I was a kid. Sure, the bird couldn't see me, but I also couldn't see him when he walked within twenty yards. I almost never got free of all those vines and thorns.

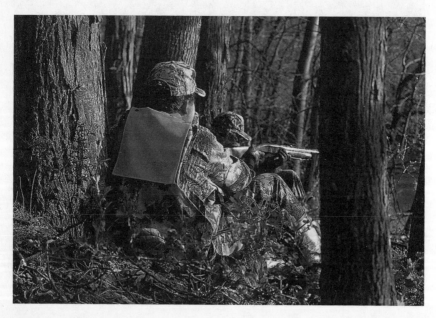

A good setup on a Missouri hardwood ridgetop. Both hunters have their backs against trees that are wider than their shoulders.

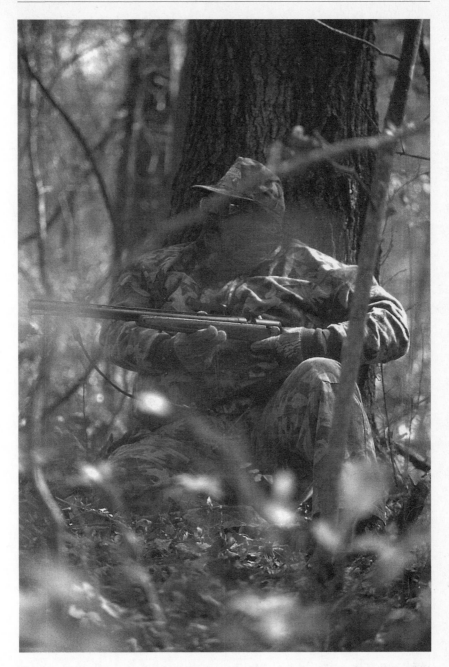

This hunter is against a tree wider than his shoulders, but the area in front is too thick with small trees and brush.

Personally, I like to sit in a kind of laid-back slouch, so that I'm low to the ground and able to keep my gun resting on my raised knees.

There are times when it's best not to call from a sitting position. Sometimes all you can do is hold your ground and pray for the best.

My dad and I managed a slow hunt on a rainy morning a few years ago. Our plan was for me to cover some ground, find a bird we could work, and then go back to get Dad so that we could set up on the bird together.

Well, events don't always unfold as planned. I heard a tom and some hens in a patch of woods near some overgrown farm fields. I circled around the open fields, hoping to get a better feel for the area and the location of the birds.

Even though I knew better, and even though I preach the contrary, I stopped while I was still essentially out in the open, behind a small tree, and gave a few cuts. The hens cut my calls and popped into view, coming over a slight rise. There I was, with nothing but an eight-inch tree between me and them.

Luckily for me, the hens were so excited that they never stopped running. When the gobbler followed them I took him with a face full of No. 6 shot. I felt like a kid with his hand in a cookie jar when Dad came up and asked who was supposed to be calling and who was supposed to be shooting.

And across much of America's turkey country there simply isn't enough underbrush to conceal a hunter sitting in front of a tree. The ponderosa pine country of the Merriam's and the cottonwood treelines of the Rios are prime examples. It's sometimes the same with easterns.

Back in 1987 I started a Massachusetts bird with an owl hoot, closed the distance, and hit him with a hen call. He gobbled right back. I circled about two hundred yards around him, but no matter where I went the woods were as open as a city park. You couldn't hide a squirrel, let alone a two-hundred-pound hunter.

Whenever I'm faced with that scenario I use what I call a blocker tree. I got on my knees behind a big hemlock, my gun pointing up. I hardly peeked around the tree.

The bird was coming in from left to right, and a couple of times I had to ease left to keep from being seen. The main problem was that there just wasn't enough cover between me and the bird for me to shoulder the gun without being seen.

After what seemed like an eternity the bird stopped behind another tree twenty-five yards away. When he stepped out I took all twenty-one pounds of him. When I stood up, I realized I had unknowingly scooted all the way around to the opposite side of the tree.

Other times you can set up against a tree knowing full well that the gobbler is going to come in behind you. In those cases, direct

A small, portable blind works well for a quick setup.

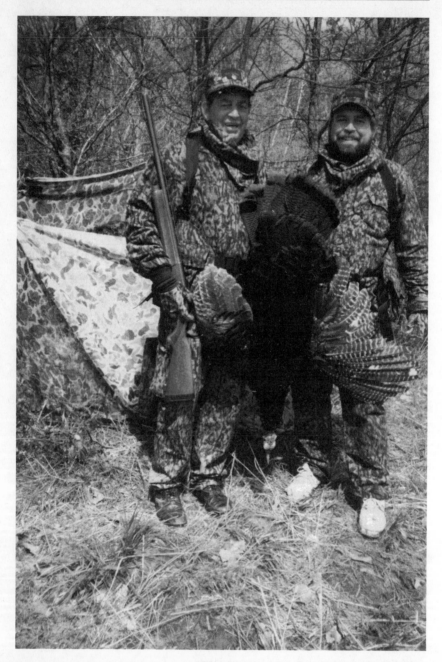

Permanent blinds in good locations are deadly. Hunting from a blind will keep pressure off your hunting area.

your calls out in front of you, then let the turkey walk right into your field of fire as he looks for the hen he thinks is still before him.

I've even killed several birds from a standing position. To do so, flatten your body against the tree as if you were a long lump in the bark; don't move until the right moment. Sometimes you can even find a tree whose branches fork at just the right height to accommodate a pointed gun.

Down in the hills where I learned much of what I use today, mostly by a little trial and a lot of error, there was an open rock glade where, sitting at the edge, you couldn't see twenty yards. But there was a Y-shaped tree growing right in front of a massive old oak that made a perfect blind. We killed a lot of turkeys looking through the branches of that old tree.

But again, calling from a sitting position in front of a tree is best. Try other postures only as last resorts.

Don't make the mistake of sitting or standing in direct sunlight. Try to find a shadow. If possible the sun should be at your back to further limit the gobbler's ability to see you.

It's a very good idea to look around and pick a landmark or two at the edge of your gun range while you're still standing. Sitting can greatly reduce your depth perception; a turkey that's twenty yards away may sometimes look as if he's twice as far off—or vice versa.

If you're right-handed, try to sit with your left shoulder pointing in the direction of the bird's approach so that you'll have a full 180-degree field of fire. Naturally, if you're left-handed you want your right side facing the bird for the best shooting.

12

LOCATING AND HUNTING STRUTTING AREAS

It's only been within the past decade that the term "strutting area" has popped into turkey hunting parlance. Actually, good turkey hunters have known about these little open pockets for generations. For me during the early days, they were just certain glades in the Ozarks where the toms came to display and gobble. For others, they might be corners of green wheat fields or flat expanses of dry land in swampy country.

No matter where, the turkeys are using them for the same basic reasons. It's not as complex or mystifying as you might think. It's simply a good place for turkeys—especially the hens.

Most strutting areas are near good nesting cover for the hens and close to greens and bugs for food. Simple biology tells you that where you find hens during breeding season you also find toms, gobbling and displaying in the open sunlight where they can be easily seen and heard.

There is a place in the east-central Missouri Ozarks where a small rocky stream winds its way past a little glade. It's met by a sloping ridge and bordered by the remnants of an ancient split rail fence. At one end, not far from the little meadow's crown, sits a mammoth oak that seems as old as the hills themselves.

Rest your back against the old tree and face the small field of spring wildflowers and growing grass and you're in one of the finest places in America to call and take a wild turkey. I know, because I've done it eight or nine times myself. From the stories I've heard, my grandfather also did it numerous times when he was a young man in the hills.

Several hundred miles to the west in the red dirt country of western Oklahoma there is a clearing that is lined by a steep canyon on one side and a scattering of brush and junipers on the other.

This place, too, is an excellent one for taking a spring tom.

Both of these secluded little spots—one in the Ozarks and the other on the prairies of Oklahoma—are productive for the same reason: they're strutting areas.

As with all spring hunting, nothing is certain and working the strutting areas succeeds only during certain times of the breeding season.

True, some toms will occasionally use a strutting area when trying to attract hens, but the best time to hunt the areas is when the mating season is either at its peak or starting its decline.

But it's never a matter of simply finding a small meadow or glade, making a few calls, then rolling a big longbeard when he runs up. There's the ever-important right time and right place to be considered first.

You probably already know what it's going to take to find such a place: scouting. Look for the usual signs of fresh tracks and droppings that seem to appear in the same location day after day. Also keep an eye out for the little ditches in the soft dirt or leaves that are left by the wingtips of a strutting turkey.

In some areas, like open farm country, it's even possible to get high on a ridge and survey the surrounding countryside for strutting gobblers. Hunters with access to a good topographic map can look for the appropriate open fields close to water and good nesting cover.

It's also possible to save a lot of walking time by listening intently for a bird that gobbles from one location all morning. If you or a friend has been working a bird that refuses to budge or that even heads in the opposite direction, there's a fair chance that he may be using his strutting area.

When you find yourself in such a situation, don't rush right after the gobbler. Take your time and get to know the terrain, even if it means waiting until later in the day. Move slowly and spend a lot of time looking and listening.

Several seasons ago I met a friend who was complaining about a bird he'd been working for several days. It was the same old story: "He'll gobble at all of my calls yet he always goes the other way, then just stays in one spot and gobbles."

These hunters, on the first morning of their hunt, took three nice gobblers out of preset blinds placed in strutting areas.

Approaching the area with the hunter, I found the perfect explanation. The tom was simply leaving the roost and heading to an old clearing where a few old hog houses sat above a nice little creek. It had all of the requirements of a good strutting area—water, good cover for nesting hens, and a high location where the gobbler could see and be seen.

We slipped into the little meadow the next morning, the hunter took a seat at the meadow's edge, and I had no problems at all calling the bird right up to him, where he took it. The bird that had frustrated him for days was one of his easiest kills once we set up on the gobbler's strutting area.

As mentioned earlier, such hotspots can be tough to find, but they're more than worth the effort. As long as there are no major changes in habitat they'll produce from year to year, decade to decade.

Just as important, though, they'll often produce day after day when one gobbler steps in to take another's place. Our guided hunters ended up taking four more longbeards off the strutting area with the old hog barns during the remaining ten days of the Missouri season.

I also watched another friend pull a miracle miss. It simply must have been an act of God: He didn't kill a huge gobbler that was standing in the open with his head periscoped up less than twenty yards away.

How and when during the day you hunt strutting areas will depend a lot on where the turkeys are in their breeding cycles and how each individual tom is acting. Many times the tom will follow the hens wherever they go in the morning. Once they're on the nest the tom prowls other strutting areas, looking for new loves.

Many times I've seen the birds roosting right at the edge of a strutting area, then using the glade for the first hour or two of daylight. In this situation the key is to move in as close as the terrain will allow before daylight, then call the bird from the roost. Even an old gobbler with four beauties on each side of him can get greedy enough to fly down a little early for some early action.

And there are also times when an area that seems devoid of turkeys early in the day will hold a strutting and gobbling tom at 10 or 11 A.M. Pay careful attention to when the birds use their strutting areas and from what direction they usually approach. Sometimes their schedules are like clockwork; and the more predictable the turkey, the easier it is to call him.

Also keep in mind that strutting areas are excellent places to try blind calling if the birds aren't gobbling. Some days even the dominant bird won't sound off even though he's strutting nearby. There's also a good chance that a subdominant bird is hanging around the area, hoping to steal a hen from the patriarch. These birds often sneak in quietly, literally looking over their shoulders for the whipping that they fear. Still, they don't want to leave the promise of a good strutting area.

The easiest way to take a turkey in a strutting area is to be there waiting for him when he appears. Chances are, if he's alone and already on the move, a little good calling can pull him right into your lap. Again, knowing the terrain and the patterns of the birds within it will tell you the time and place for calling.

Always remember to be careful when approaching a strutting area. One reason the birds like these areas so much is that they can see not only hens, but also predators. Use the terrain to block your approach, and take some time to study the field for turkeys with each step.

Taking a bird that's already set up can be a real challenge. If the bird has hens feeding around him he probably won't want to leave them. When such is the case forget about the tom and start working on the hens.

Try to get the dominant hen fired up with aggressive cutting and yelps. Once she opens up, really pour it on. If she comes, the flock will probably follow, including the strutting gobbler.

Sometimes you can figure out a way to split the tom from the hens and then set up to call the old bird right in. I use such a tactic only as a last resort. It's usually better to study the birds and either wait until the hens leave or come back earlier the next morning, changing your calling position to the place where the tom and hens were strutting.

It can also be awfully difficult to pull a lone gobbler from the middle of a strutting area to a place where you can shoot him. If a gobbler is in a position where he can see well he may wait until the hen shows herself. Sometimes you can hide behind a slight rise in elevation to fool the gobbler into thinking there's a hen just out of sight. Other times you can either turn and send your calls over your shoulder or ask your buddy to walk off, calling like a hen playing hard to get.

And never forget the aggressive calls, such as excited hen calls and hard gobbler yelping and cutting. Get a big gobbler, or any other turkey that's in the area, fired up near a strutting area and you may see the show of your life.

A few days after I found the strutting area near the hog barn, Butch Milne and I were stood up by hunters we were supposed to guide. Not wanting to let a good morning go to waste we headed into the woods just as day was breaking.

Butch set out toward a gobble from the northwest while I headed in the general location of the strutting area. I didn't need to hoot to get the birds to gobble; they were cutting loose on their own. From the sounds of things they were still on the roost.

The spreading light meant that I couldn't move in and set up as usual; so I stayed back a little and tried to plan an approach that would get me close to the birds' roost. Using a ring of cedars for cover, I moved toward where the birds were talking.

By then it was so light that some of the hens were flying down, and the gobbler in the tree was gobbling at everything—owl hoots, crows, barking squirrels, hen calls, and especially the gobbles of another tom in a valley to the east.

I somehow managed to work my way close to the roost tree without being seen. I made a soft call and the tom went crazy as several more hens pitched out of the tree and landed just a few feet from where I sat.

I figured the big bird would follow the ladies and the hunt would be over in a matter of seconds—but that wasn't the case. The gobbler sailed down but headed toward the other tom at a dead run, sending challenging gobbles with almost every step.

All I could do was sit there, as motionless as a camouflaged stump while I listened to the excited hen talk and the loud noises of two toms fighting it out eighty yards away.

When the fight was over the hens set out across a shallow, gravel-bottomed creek in single file, moving like one long, feathered snake up a winding trail toward the old pig barns. They passed so close I could hear their low putts and the soft sounds of their feet on the damp leaves.

The gobbler didn't respond to my soft calling, so I hurried north to set up where I knew the birds were headed. Easing up to the edge of the strutting area, I couldn't see any turkeys. I crawled to some rocks and small cedars and looked again. This time I could see him in full strut, surrounded by hens at the other end of the glade sixty yards away.

Staying low, I gave a few soft hen calls. A couple of hens yelped back. The birds were at that awkward distance that's out of range yet too close to call loudly or move an inch. I buried my face in my chest and tried some fighting purrs and putts. Hens started racing back and forth, and the tom slowly moved closer in full strut.

I waited a while and tried some soft gobbler yelps. Again the bird gobbled, as did another tom that sounded to be about 150 yards behind me. The tom on the glade slowed, yet kept gobbling while the bird behind me rapidly closed the distance.

Meanwhile there I sat, in a small cluster of stones and bushes that didn't seem big enough to hide a bird dog, let alone a full-grown man.

By now the early morning sun had spread across the glade, causing the tom in front of me to glow as he strutted forty yards away. From the gobbles and drumming it sounded as if the gobbler behind me was only half as far off. I knew I couldn't move.

Even after the tom I was watching had closed into gun range I couldn't fire for fear of hitting one of the dozen or more hens surrounding him. So I waited, fully expecting to hear the loud alarm putts of the turkey behind me when he finally made out my shape. There was also another hen coming in from my left that could be a problem.

Finally one of the hens stopped and squatted; the old gobbler mounted her. The rest of the hens spread out a little, putting softly and running about the area. The whole thing seemed almost magical in the early morning light, the birds glistening and their shadows stretching across the glade.

The bred hen finally scurried from beneath the gobbler, causing him to stand and shake his feathers back into position. I putted and he stretched his head up one last time. The bird had spurs that were 1½ inches long.

I was still kneeling over the bird when the sound of a shot rolled in from Butch's direction. I sat on the glade for close to an hour, just enjoying the morning and the quality of the bird, and thinking of the good times the strutting area would hold in the future.

Unfortunately that strutting area is gone now, thanks to intensive lumbering and mining. But there are other strutting areas, and they will offer other memories yet to be made.

13

HENNED-UP GOBBLERS

Years ago, in the early years of the restoration program in Missouri, it was not uncommon to hear a tom at very first light sound off, fly down, and gobble all day. That same bird moved miles through the mountains looking for hens.

With the success of wild turkey programs all across America, there are turkeys in just about every available habitat. Large numbers of healthy turkeys means more hens; more hens means more competition for the gobblers. Gobblers today do not have to travel to find hens; they usually wake up with them. With all the available girls, it's less gobbling and more intense strutting and displaying. This is something hunters all across America's turkey country are talking about. "The gobblers aren't responding". . . "They're still with the hens." Or they're "henned up." It is a very common problem today. For one thing, in addition to more hens, spring seasons are set months or years in advance; a late spring will often find the tom courting the ladies that come running to him instead of going out to look for another party.

There are several signs that gobblers are with hens. Some are obvious: seeing them together in open fields, or hearing the hens yelping and cutting around the gobbler on the roost.

Other possible indications are toms that gobble well on the roost, but then go silent when they've gathered their hens soon after flying down. Sometimes birds that respond but won't come in may already be with hens. Many hunters blame their calling, but you can't expect a gobbler to leave a sure thing for a blind date in the bush, even if she does sound as if she has a great personality.

Whenever I find myself competing with the real thing I usually forget all about the tom and start working on his hens. Bring them in, and you can almost always count on the gobbler following them step for step.

The first thing you must realize is that talking with a hen is quite different from talking to a gobbler. You're sending completely different messages. While you're promising love to the gobbler, you're telling the hen that you're a new girl and you've come to take her date.

The key is to get her responding, and then imitate what she does, only more aggressively with each conversation. If she yelps six times, you yelp eight times with just a little more feeling. If she starts cutting, you're in business.

Several years ago a client and I were well back into the Ozarks on a late-spring morning that had the gobblers surrounded by harems of willing hens. We'd failed to find a bird to work on the roost, and our moving and calling hadn't gone well either.

Then about 10 A.M. I got a single gobble. A little later a hen answered from the same direction. From then on the tom never made another sound, and the hen uttered only an occasional yelp. Realizing the problem for what it was, I went after the hen with aggressive calling. Eventually the hen answered my challenge with excited cutting. Almost immediately three or four other hens joined in. A couple of gobblers in different locations also entered into the shouting match.

The dominant hen finally made her move, running up the hill to our right, cutting and putting with every step. The rest of the hens—seven in all—were close behind.

My hunter did an excellent job of holding still and watching as the hens ran right past where we sat. A few seconds later came the big gobbler, strutting a few short steps, then hurrying to catch up. He never caught up.

I use this anecdote because it shows that it is possible to call hens, or even a group of them. Not a season passes that I don't bring in a tom simply by challenging his hens. There's no doubt in my mind that more good callers could do the same if they'd just develop the skills, then use them at the right time.

Sure, sometimes you call in hens that don't have a gobbler, but it's worth trying. Hold your ground, don't be afraid to call aggressively, and be alert. Remember that a few hunters out there are foolish enough to call as they sneak up on hen calls, so be alert and make positive identification.

I've killed a lot of gobblers that were with hens by relying on one of the gobbler's most predictable traits—a greed for sex. It's often possible to move in close to a bird that's roosted with hens and call him in as soon as he flies down.

As mentioned earlier, sneak in quietly well before fly-down time. Get as close as possible; if you have done your scouting, you will set up in his fly-down area.

The second you hear drumming on the limb or the first gobble of the day, give a few soft tree yelps. When it is light enough to see about thirty yards, increase the intensity of your calls. If you're set up where he gathers his hens, there's a strong chance that the gobbler might just fly down to get things started early.

Another tactic I use is to separate the gobbler from his hens. The odds should rapidly swing to your favor. If the gobbler's having

During this hunt, hens were challenged with aggressive cutting and yelping. The two nice gobblers followed the hens right to the hunters.

the time of his life for days with the hens and then suddenly finds himself a bachelor, that tom usually won't waste any time trying to get romancing again.

It's often possible to sneak up on a roosted flock and scare them by running at them, clapping, barking like a dog, or making some other noise. The key is to get close enough to force a good scatter. If the gobbler flies off with his hens you're no better off than before. But make him spend the night alone on a limb and he'll probably go berserk. The same scattering method works at sunrise as well.

If you've scattered the birds the night before, move in and work the tom from the limb the next morning. That gobbler should be more than ready to get back to the girls. If you make a dawn scatter, let the woods settle for a few minutes, then call from a position between the gobbler and the hens—maybe even right at the roost. Be prepared for a bird that may literally run into your lap.

In the right situation you can fool a bird that's been snubbing your hen calls by hitting him with some gobbler talk. There was a time in my life when I killed a lot of dominant gobblers by gobbling at them with my voice. Let me tell you, it is an exciting and real experience to call a gobbler that comes in for a fight. Be somewhat careful using the gobble on state or national forest land, areas full of overanxious hunters. If you cannot gobble with your voice, there are some good gobble calls available; HS Strut comes to mind. An alternative to gobbling, and much easier to duplicate, is gobbler yelping.

I remember toms that refused to budge at a hen call racing out to whip a yelping jake.

If you pay attention in the woods you'll hear both jakes and mature toms yelp, cut, purr, and make many of the same calls as hens. The difference is how they sound. There are exceptions, but most gobblers and jakes have a slower rhythm; their calls have fewer notes and are more drawn out than hen talk. Gobbler talk also seems to be a little deeper in pitch and sometimes raspier than hens.

Some hunters may look on these gobbler calls as secondary tools, something nice to know but seldom used. In a way it's just the opposite. When the conditions are right—during the mating season—hen talk can be dynamite, but at other times it can be a bust.

But gobblers talk tom to tom twelve months out of the year. I've been calling gobblers in with gobbler talk during all four seasons for the past thirty-something years.

Gobbler yelps work for the same reason calling hen to hen works. The toms have a set pecking order, and if you try to squeeze into it, some birds are going to get upset. Try using jake yelps when the mature birds are gobbling at each other and setting their pecking order.

Believe me, there are times when a hen yelp just won't work, but gobbler yelping and cutting will bring the woods to life. A few seasons back a friend and I found ourselves working a tom that wouldn't leave his hens to cross a clearing to where we sat.

I had started off slow and easy, eventually building to some of my most aggressive hen cutting—but still no response. A few minutes later I let loose some gobbler yelps and cutting, and another bird opened up with the same thing back behind us. I wasted no time coming back a little longer and louder. With all of the gobbler talk the bird across the clearing started going crazy.

Both toms broke, left the hens, and ran at us at full speed. One gobbled every step, and the other yelped as many as twenty times in a row with some strings of seven or eight cuts mixed in. My hunter friend killed the gobbling bird as he charged right at us.

As you can see, there are several ways to get around the gobbler-with-hens problem. The main idea is to accept the challenge and try something other than mating yelps.

And don't make the mistake of giving up too early. All turkeys go through the breeding cycle differently. While one tom may have a dozen hens, there may be a subdominant one just over the next ridge that doesn't have any.

Additionally, it's not at all uncommon for a tom to breed all of his hens early in the morning, then go looking for more later in the morning while the hens are on the nest.

If you work a bird at daybreak but can't get him into gun range, go back three or four hours later and give him a whirl. I've had a lot of these birds run right in to my first set of calls the second time around.

14

TACTICS FOR LATE SPRING

Most game commissions attempt to set their spring season to coincide with the spring mating season and when most of the hen population is on the nest. Some years things work out and other years Mother Nature just does not cooperate. A late spring is one of the most common problems turkey hunters face. A turkey hunter should be willing to make changes and adjust his tactics depending on the weather and the cycle of the birds in the area hunted.

I've already mentioned such things as blind calling, using gobbler yelps, and handling toms that are with hens. One problem that can't be ignored is the lack of cover. I've seen a lot of spring seasons with no more underbrush than there was in December. The lack of cover means you're going to be exposed for a much greater distance. Over the years I heard a lot of complaints from hunters during a late spring. They spoke of birds gobbling, but going silent when the hunter moved into a calling position. Personally, I think a lot of hunters were being seen in those open woods

When the woods are open, with little or no green-up, it's important to keep your distance from a bird you're working. We had to set

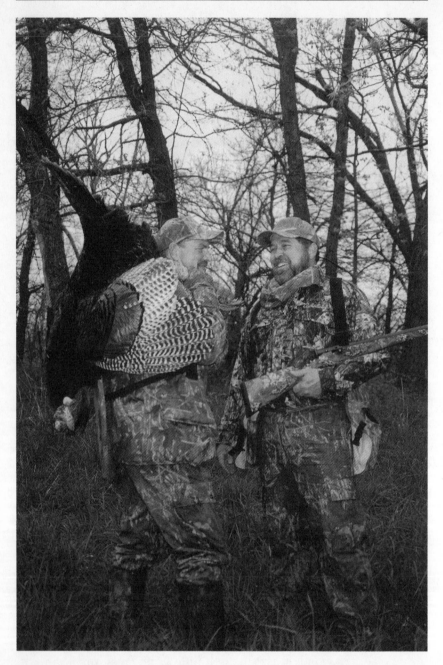

During a late spring, utilize the pecking order and challenge the toms. Gobblers were still running together. This late spring gobbler was taken by gobbler yelping.

up close to a quarter of a mile away from the first gobbler that I called in for my brother Marty when he was a little boy. The woods were so barren that we watched the bird come the last two hundred yards.

If possible, try to keep some obstruction like the break of a ridge or a blowdown between you and the bird. It's also good to set up behind trees rather than in front of them.

You also have to adapt your calling. Locating calls aren't going to work well, and most of the calling that the turkeys do will be from gobbler to gobbler.

Keep your ears open for things other than gobbles and yelps. The sounds of two gobblers flapping and fighting carry for a long distance on still mornings. What that sound tells me is that there are at least two gobblers within hearing distance, their emotions are running high, and they're paying attention to something other than me.

I like to try to move in close to fighting gobblers. Once I hear the fight I'm up and moving in a hurry, since they can't hear or see well during the commotion. It may surprise you just how close you can get to fighting gobblers. The key is to waste no time, get close, and get ready.

I'll never forget the morning a hunter and I walked our tails into the ground before we heard two birds gobbling at each other from adjoining ridges. I did my best to stir things up with aggressive calls. We hurried up an old logging road in hopes of intercepting the birds that were gobbling nonstop, but we got there too late.

One of the gobblers had crossed over to the other ridge and the fight was on. We could hear them thumping and flapping; so we wasted little time slipping over the saddle of the ridge and sneaked to within forty-five yards of the melee.

After a few minutes nonstop fighting the toms rushed over the edge of the ridge, and the loser flushed and sailed away across the valley The other tom, the winner, went into a quick strut and sounded a triumphant gobble. I gave a few aggressive calls, hen and gobbler yelps, and the bird came strutting right toward us with aggressive purring and putting. The bird, at about ten yards, assumed a fighting posture. He lost the second fight.

If the spring is really late you may find yourself facing winter flocks of gobblers. In such a situation, use fall calling tactics. You can lure flocks with gobbler yelps and cuts, or you can split the flock and go after both halves.

The second year outdoor writer Mike Pearce and I hunted together, the Missouri woods were barren and the gobblers still flocked up. About 8 A.M. that morning I got onto a flock of eight or ten gobblers, eventually pulled them into range, and shot a longbeard, thus scattering the rest of the flock.

Half an hour or so later Mike circled back into the area to find me. I immediately sent him off the ridge in the direction of the scatter. Stopping at the edge of a large glade, he gave a few pleading, drawn-out gobbler yelps. A gobbler responded. Before it was over he had five toms closing in from three different directions yelping, cutting, and gobbling. The one he tagged tipped the scales at twenty-two pounds.

Taking a spring gobbler is a challenge anytime, let alone when Mother Nature throws you a curve. But remember that the longer and harder you hunt, the higher your chances for success.

15

HUNTING IN BAD WEATHER

Spring turkey season is a special time of year, a very short period of time when the woods come back to life, wild turkeys gobble and strut all across America, and the age-old ritual of the mating season takes place. Hunters ask, "What is the best time to hunt turkeys?" My answer is always the same: When the season is open, regardless of the weather, a hunter must take advantage of every day available to be consistently successful. It is quite simple; the harder you hunt, the more time you spend in the woods, the better the odds you will kill a turkey.

WIND

Without a doubt a turkey hunter's biggest enemy is the wind. Turkey hunters rely on hearing and on being heard, both of which become very difficult in any wind at all.

Here again, it's important to scout so that you hunt where there are turkeys. Try to find a place that's out of the wind, like valleys and the windless sides of hills.

Take your time and work the area well. Don't travel far between setups, keep the wind at your back, and allow the wind to carry your calling to the turkeys. Stay longer on blind-calling setups than you would on a calm day. Set up where you can see more area. Use your loud box call, and make all calls loud. You can strain your ears into the wind, but you're better off to watch for the approach of a turkey.

Turkeys hear far better than any of us, especially with the wind at our backs. On a day when the wind was twisting the Oklahoma cottonwoods to their roots, I watched a gobbler respond to every one of my calls from a hundred yards away as his head snapped out to gobble, but I never heard a note.

Be careful of your reaction when you do hear a bird respond. If you hear a gobble, sit down quickly; the bird is probably very close. Because a heavy wind will distort calls, you may not be certain of a tom's exact location until you see him. It also works the other way around: The gobbler may have a little trouble pinpointing the location of your calling. Be patient and don't give up until the second you have to head for home. I've never experienced a wind strong enough to blow the turkeys away. Well, then again, maybe I have, but I was out there with the turkeys.

RAIN

The rain began sometime during the night and seemed as though it intended to stay for a while. It was still coming down in a steady pour when I pulled my hat down tight and headed down the ridge. A gobbler answered my first hoots.

The turkey acted as if it was a beautiful, seventy-degree morning, gobbling at my hoots and loud yelps. The gobbler flew down, hit the ground gobbling, and headed toward me at a dead run, and I mean a dead run. The shot was less than twenty yards. I took my time leaving the woods, despite the continuing rain.

To be honest, I can't help but smile when I remember rainy-day turkey hunts. Like turkeys, no two such hunts have been alike except that there have been darned few that haven't produced their share of excitement.

But maybe one of the key reasons I like hunting in the rain is that it drives most hunters—some would say the most sensible hunters—from the woods. There's something special in knowing you're the only one around as you move silently over a dampened carpet of leaves.

It can also be a prime time to call and kill turkeys. Birds can't retreat to pickups or coffee shops. Rain is as much a part of their lives as sunshine and wind. Except in weather just short of a hurricane, they continue to move and feed in the rain. They'll gobble and respond to calls; it's just another day in the turkey world.

There are dozens of anecdotes I could choose from, but when I think of hunting in the rain my mind always fixes on a hunt I had with Pat Leonard. It wasn't just raining. It was flat out pouring all morning. We couldn't have been any wetter as we sloshed our way around the hardwood hills.

But our main problem was trying to hear—and be heard—in the rain. It pounded down so hard that it deadened any calls, both the birds' and ours. Still, we continued to move and call. Yanking a box call out of a bread wrapper, we huddled over it long enough to cut loose a long and loud series of calls before shoving it back into my pocket.

Walking and calling, we weren't expecting to hear anything. Suddenly what sounded like a gobble cut through the roar of pouring water and we looked at each other, neither one wanting to say anything until we were sure the other had heard the same thing. I took the call back out, hit a few more licks, and this time there was no mistaking the gobble. We set up with our backs against big trees while rain ran like waterfalls over the bills of our hats. Before long not one, but two gobblers came in, gobbling and strutting as if it were a still and sunny morning. Rounding a tree, the birds raised their heads, then fell as two shots sounded as one.

Whether or not you want to sit in the rain is up to you, but I don't think anyone should miss the half hour before a storm system moves in. I can remember sitting on the mountain above my grandfather's place, watching a front approach from dozens of miles away. So many times woods that had sat silent since daybreak would come alive with the first distant rumblings of thunder. The closer the storm got, the more intense became the gobbling.

There were many times that we'd pile off the mountaintop, set up on a bird, take him, and still be back at the homestead for the first taps of rain on the old tin roof.

Even if you choose to sit out a shower, it's often best to stay in the area. Take a nap in your truck, but don't miss what might become a good day to hunt. Gobblers get as excited at the end of a rainstorm (or even just a lull between two storms) as they do at a system's approach. Find yourself in the woods at such a time, and your chances for hearing gobblers are as good as at daybreak.

Early one morning I drove my old '64 GMC truck into the timber on a stormy morning that had put most creeks over their banks. Even the old two-track logging road that I followed from the main road was running like twin rivers in the beams of my headlights.

Between the wind and the rain, visibility couldn't have been more than a couple of hundred feet at daybreak. That, plus bolt after bolt of lightning, caused me to think twice about going in at that time. Within minutes I was asleep in the cab of my truck.

When I awoke, the wind had died and the rain had softened to a gentle shower. Rolling down the window of the truck, I could hear the sound of turkeys gobbling all across the mountain. I hurried to the closest bird, set up in a good calling position, fired him up, and took him when he came up. The torrents of rain hit again just as I made it back to the truck.

The key to hunting in the rain is to rely on your common sense. If you have decent rain equipment and there's no lightning, then maybe you should hunt. Today's raingear is much better than just a few short years ago. My Cabela's raingear not only keeps me dry, it is quiet and comfortable. Another option is hunting from a blind with a roof. Today's blinds will keep you dry and warm on a rainy day. A good blind set up on a field edge, a good strutting or feeding area, is very deadly, and you can pack a lunch and stay all day. Don't get discouraged if the birds aren't gobbling. A lot of bad-weather toms come in silently. But they still come to calls. After all, they only get to play this mating game for a few weeks of the year and they're not likely to let a little water get in their way. As I see it, neither will most good turkey hunters.

SNOW

A slow, steady rain made for a slippery climb as John Hauer and I left his Suburban and hiked up into the Black Hills. By the time we reached the top of the ridge the raindrops were bigger, splatting down in the form of slush.

We continued along the ridge, stopping every so often to send a series of calls down the slopes. By the time we reached our third or fourth calling position it was beginning to snow. The longer we hunted the harder it fell.

Two hours after dawn a bird gobbled, and I started calling from behind a huge ponderosa. Two toms, a jake, and a mature bird came over the lip of the ridge, the bigger bird strutting for all he was worth.

But then it hit me. Because of the treacherous walking I hadn't moved a shell from my magazine to the chamber of my shotgun. By some minor miracle I managed to accomplish that task, but when I took aim, the jake spooked and the big gobbler ducked out of sight.

By then it was snowing hard, with flakes the size of quarters dropping from the sky. After a good laugh at my forgetfulness, Hauer and I moved to the next ridge and set up. This time there was no gobble, just three red and blue heads coming over the ridge after my first series of calls.

We were now sitting in what was becoming a full-fledged blizzard. I took the first tom to offer a clear shot and we headed off the hill, leaving tracks in the snow behind us.

As you can see, turkey hunting in snow has never really posed many problems for me, or for other hunters like Hauer who have to deal with it every year. For most hunters it's little more than a temporary freak of nature, a phenomenon that will pass in a few hours. Several Missouri openers have seen up to three inches of snow, yet thousands of hunters still take birds.

Depending on the conditions, sometimes the toms gobble as if all is normal. Other times they play the game quietly, coming to calls without gobbling or with just a few gobbler yelps.

Snow is like any other weather-related problem, in that you have to realize the limitations and keep hunting. If the birds aren't gobbling well, then set up and blind-call in some of your favored locations. If they don't respond to spring calls, try fall calls like gobbler yelps.

Keep trying and sooner or later you'll succeed, something you can't do from the warm confines of a camper or coffee shop.

16

HUNTING PRESSURED BIRDS

The opening day of turkey season finally arrives; you're driving to that little secluded place on the back edge of the national forest. You're thinking about all the gobbling you heard while scouting that big ridge to the north. All that excitement and anticipation come crashing down as you pull into what you thought was your secret little spot. Four trucks are parked, and a fifth truck is driving right up the road to your ridge.

With today's soaring popularity of turkey hunting there's going to be a lot more competition in the woods—especially on public ground. Knowing the woods and the turkeys within them can be more critical than ever on heavily hunted grounds. Try to be in close and waiting when that gobbler pitches off the roost. Also, identify the areas with the most hunting pressure. Look for little, out-of-the-way pockets of timber and make the extra effort to stay away from other hunters—for their sake as well as yours.

It's also wise to change the hunt pattern. If most hunters are parking on one stretch of road and walking in from the east, then find a way to come in from the west.

Sometimes it's possible to float a canoe into desolate back-country that's free of hunters. Other times you have to take a boat across a lake to get the surrounding woods all to yourself. Some national forests also allow you to backpack to areas too remote for most hunters. Remember, the main goal is to be unique, to keep from blending into the crowd of hunters. I avoid hunting weekends and opening days on public ground. I've also returned to places on a weekday late in the season and have had an entire national forest pretty much to myself.

The same thing goes for time of day as well. The woods may be packed at sunrise but nearly free of hunters by ten or eleven that morning. Also, if you think most hunters are hen yelping on dia-phragm calls, then try cutting and purring on a box or slate call, and don't forget the gobbler yelps.

Several years ago David Crowe of Alabama and I headed into a heavily hunted state forest about an hour and a half before the noon quitting time.

My preseason scouting revealed a dominant bird working a long ridge. Unfortunately the road beside the ridge looked like a parking lot most early mornings. We quietly worked our way to the heart of the bird's territory, lay down, and took a short nap to get some much-needed rest. A little later, the sound of one of the last trucks driving away echoed through the valley. I waited a few min-utes for the woods to settle down, then softly yelped on my favorite old slate call. After several long minutes the bird gobbled. I yelped back more aggressively; the bird gobbled, but did not sound very in-terested. I switched to my voice to gobbler yelp aggressively; I walked the opposite way from both hunter and bird, mixing hen yelps with gobbler yelps as I walked.

The gobbler weighed 23½ pounds, with an 11½-inch beard and 1½-spurs.

Working birds that have been spooked several times for days on

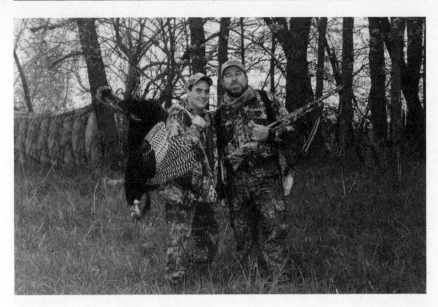

This hunting area is extremely open, and hunting from blinds eliminated pressure on the turkeys. A turkey hunter should be willing to change and adapt to the situation.

A canoe is an excellent way to reach birds far back in the woods. Where legal, it is also good for floating rivers, stopping often to listen and call for gobblers.

end often means using a lot more patience and a slightly different style of calling. I usually move shorter distances and stay longer. It also helps to keep the calls a little softer, imitating a hen that's just as nervous as the gobbler. Sometimes I scratch the leaves with my hands to further convince an old gobbler that I'm a real hen. If the tom's real close, I may just simply scratch the leaves.

Where there's lots of pressure from hunters, you can expect less gobbling and toms that often simply show up when you're blind calling. Keep in mind that gobbling brings competition; don't encourage it. I seldom use locating calls on crowded hunting areas.

Also, it's important that you know how to deal with other hunters in the area. Place hunter orange behind your setup. If a hunter comes in on a bird that you're working, do not make any unnecessary movement, just talk in a loud calm voice to let him know you are there. I've taken several spooked birds by waiting fifteen to thirty minutes, then calling softly like a nervous hen.

A friend and I once found several vehicles parked near a really good bird's territory in a small patch of timber between a river and a major county road. Knowing that the bird was probably already spooked, we headed to town for breakfast.

At half past ten we cruised the area and noted that the cars were gone. We parked well down the road and quietly circled back to the place I'd heard the gobbler before the season. Again, I opted for a slate call and some very light clucks and purrs followed by some yelps. The bird gobbled only once, but he walked right up to Jack, who took him.

It's important to keep in mind that there are other hunters in the woods. There are times when you may want to go to some lengths to keep other hunters from working or spooking your bird. One night two of us intentionally spooked an old double-beard from his roost near two well-traveled roads.

At daylight several trucks stopped, hooted or crow called, then left when they got no response. We, on the other hand, set up right at the original roost tree and used hen calls to bring the bird into gun range.

But you need to keep things in perspective when you're in the woods with a lot of other hunters. If the ground is public, or even if it's private and other hunters have permission, they have just as much right to be there as you do.

If you hear others working a bird, sit tight and see what happens. Don't spook the bird someone's working just so he can't have a chance at it. There are more than enough turkeys to go around. And as always, be careful and think of safety at all times.

17

WHEN TOMS WON'T COME IN

When everything is just right, the weather is good, and you're hunting the high peak of gobbling, and most of the hens are on the nest, you could probably squeak a barbed wire fence and call in a gobbler from four hundred yards. Yes, that would be pretty nice in a perfect turkey world, but seldom is this the case. As you well know, gobblers do not always just break and run to the sounds of a spring hen. There are so many reasons and variables to why a gobbler does not come to a hunter's call, or comes part of the way and then does what hunters commonly call "hang up." Yes, as it usually goes, events don't progress as planned in the turkey woods. The hunts we dream about—birds gobbling at anything and running right to calls—are usually in the minority.

But success can still be yours, with a little understanding. Remember one thing, the turkeys make the rules. Basically, they live there and come and go as they please; they go uphill, downhill, fly rivers, and only a turkey knows why he does or does not come to a call.

One of the most exciting, yet most frustrating, experiences is working a bird that gobbles at every one of your calls, but won't come in. Sometimes he'll cover part of the distance; sometimes he won't budge an inch, and sometimes he'll even head directly away from you, still gobbling at every call you make. Talking with hundreds of frustrated hunters, I've decided that it is possible poor calling position is to blame for the majority of hang-ups. Many may be attributed to fences, deep ditches, creeks, highways, thick brush, or anything else that a gobbler simply at that time doesn't want to cross.

The easiest cure for such hang-ups is to eliminate them before they happen. Get as close as the terrain will allow and make it as easy as possible for the turkey to get to you.

But there are also times when a gobbler simply wants to hold his ground, probably waiting for the hen to come to him. Often changing calls or callers, and throwing out something a little different will make the difference on such a bird.

The tom that's standing just out of gun range may come on in if he hears a little different-sounding hen. Just the reverse may work on the gobbler that stays in one spot farther away: Hit him with some hot cutting and he just might get excited, break, and come on in.

There have been times when I've turned my head and called, imitating a hen walking away by throwing the sound. Gobblers often go berserk and come sprinting in. There have been times when I go silent for fifteen to twenty minutes to bring an uncooperative bird right in. In addition, I've used jake yelping to get a dominant gobbler so mad that he has to come over to fight and run the jake away.

The main idea is to feel free to try something a little different if what you've been doing isn't working.

No matter why a bird won't come in—if there's a barrier in his way or he's just being bullheaded—you may see him come right on in if you simply change locations and change calls.

It's tough to tell when to move on a gobbling bird. I've moved at the wrong time, only to see the bird gobbling from my former location within a minute after my departure.

But if the bird is definitely heading the other way or hasn't moved any closer for quite some time, then it might be time to ease into a new location.

Back away from where you were calling and go around the bird. If the bird is leaving and going in a set direction, then I quietly hustle around until I'm ahead of him, then try him again. Get between him and his destination and the odds are in your favor.

Sometimes all you have to do is set up on another side of the bird, especially if the turkey acts like he would rather not cross some obstacle.

If you hunt long enough, you'll run across a gobbler that's totally uncooperative; or maybe he won't come because he simply doesn't want to. Maybe he's doing something you do not know about, what he does every day, going to some hens. All you can do is go to another bird or keep trying with the same one. Sometimes persistence pays off.

One particular hunt I will always remember happened some twenty-six years ago. I set up on a gobbler on a morning cold enough that my Jeep broke through ice in the mud holes as I followed a curving, rough route to the top of an Ozark mountain.

I eased the Jeep to a stop not far from where a saddle and a series of glades joined this mountain with another. Through the years it had been a place to hear a number of gobblers, but on that frosty morning there was but a single tom gobbling. But oh, was he ever gobbling.

I started him on the limb with a hoot, and he gobbled at it. He gobbled at every one of my hen calls, but when he hit the ground he wouldn't budge an inch. It didn't matter whether I used my voice, slate, diaphragm, or box call; the bird wouldn't come in. Then again he wouldn't shut up, either. He gobbled at every call I made.

We traded calls for about forty-five minutes before the gobbler slowly started moving away. I made a move, circling around the ridge. I set up about seventy yards out and called with my box call; he gobbled but wouldn't move. Then he started moving again, in a different direction.

I moved four more times on this bird and always had the same reaction. I tried calling nearly nonstop and I tried total silence, but he wouldn't begin to come in. No matter where I set up, he slowly moved away.

I made the decision to try one more time. Moving in at about the same level, I made a soft voice tree call. The bird turned and sprinted right to me.

As far as I know, the twenty-two-pound tom with inch-plus spurs hadn't seen hunters that season, he didn't have any hens with him, and I know that I never spooked him. So it goes with turkeys; I have never had two act exactly alike. It just goes to show you, never give up.

18

DEALING WITH SILENT BIRDS

The booming call of the wild spring gobbler is the sound that turkey hunters wait for all year, a sound all turkey hunters live for. Wherever you may hunt spring turkeys, it is all part of the game; some days toms just do not gobble. Sometimes it is weather related, other times it may be too much pressure on an area. If you're hunting the peak of the mating period, toms are busy and have no time or need to gobble. With turkey populations at an all-time high, toms do not have to gobble much to find hens. More hens means less gobbling, more strutting. Many tactics already covered in this book can be employed, such as calling hens, hunting a strutting area, or challenging a tom with gobbler yelping.

No matter what tactic or call you use, remember that just because you don't hear a gobble doesn't mean a bird will not respond to your calls. The same goes for birds that are under a lot of pressure or not at the peak of the breeding season. They are still turkeys and will act like turkeys. No matter what the reason, if birds aren't gobbling, your best bet is to move and blind call. I hate to sound like a broken record, but if possible stick to the high country where you

This adult gobbler came in silently, late in the morning. The hunter called him into gun range by moving from position to position throughout his hunting area.

can be heard, and go where your scouting has proven there are gobblers.

Knowing how long to sit in one place, though, is the big question and it's one that I can't definitely answer. I've sat in one place for an hour without seeing or hearing anything, then flushed a bird that was coming in the second I stood up.

If you have a lot of confidence in an area and the birds simply aren't gobbling, it doesn't hurt to blind call for thirty to forty-five minutes. If one spot doesn't pan out, then keep moving until you've covered your entire hunting area. The important thing is to keep a positive attitude and your senses on full alert at all times.

Listen for sounds like turkeys walking and gobblers spitting and drumming. Pay attention to the wildlife around you. The scolding of squirrels, crows, and blue jays may reveal the location of an approaching gobbler.

Keep your eyes open for any sign of turkeys moving in your direction, no matter how bored or miserable you are. Several years ago one of the few days I didn't have someone to call for dawned cloudy and cold, with a slushy snow that soaked everything. The first area was totally silent except for the sounds of dripping water and the occasional chatter of my teeth as I tried spot after spot to no avail.

By midmorning I was thawing out in my Jeep as I headed toward the country I know better than any other—the national forest I roamed as a boy, near my grandfather's farm.

Things didn't look too promising as I slipped and slid my way around the hills. The area had been hunted hard, and the birds weren't gobbling well when it was warm and sunny, let alone freezing cold and overcast.

My first two setups were total busts, which only got me soaked and shivering again. Calling position number three was a series of small, overgrown fields that sat nestled between a jagged series of ridges.

I'd been there what seemed like ten hours, probably closer to ten minutes, and was just about to pack it in for good when something out of the ordinary caught my ear. I sat silently and strained my ears. There it was again—the low, vibrating noise of a drumming gobbler. I slipped out a few more soft notes and then shut up.

Staring out into the gloom, I could barely make out the tops of five adult turkey fans coming over a slight rise in front of me. Except for the drumming, the gobblers moved as silently as ghosts as they closed the distance. The longbeard I took from the bunch was far from my biggest, but he's darned sure one of my most memorable.

19

DOUBLING UP

Team hunting can be very successful. With two experienced hunters and callers, two well-worn turkey guns, and a good game plan many, many turkeys are carried out of the woods each and every year. However, the thing I enjoy the most about doubling up on turkeys is the opportunity to teach and hunt with a new hunter; adult or youth, it does not matter. Sharing with others what you have learned turkey hunting is a great feeling. I have always enjoyed sharing the excitement with someone taking his or her first turkey, much more than shooting a bird myself. Once a hunter has some experience and would like to continue learning while hunting on their own, turkey hunting is best as a solitary sport. Your chances for success are far better when you can move quietly and without delay, making all your own decisions. Two people walking in the woods make as much noise as three or four. And you also have to worry about what the other hunter is doing or thinking.

However, I also feel you have a moral obligation to double up when you're with a hunter who is new to the sport. Turkey hunting can be frustrating enough for veterans, let alone someone new. I encourage all good hunters to share a little of what they've learned with

Turkey hunting is usually done solo, but there are times when the buddy system works well. When calling for someone with experience, the caller should move and call behind the hunter. With inexperienced hunters, the caller should set up with them.

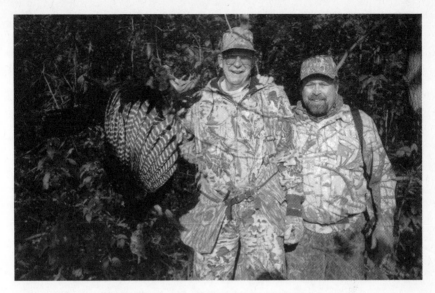

Calling a turkey for someone else can be as much fun as hunting for yourself.

beginners. If an experienced hunter has a close friend or relative who's new to the sport, he may want to take him along on a hunt or two.

Most of the time the hunt involves having one hunter and one shooter. In other words, the more experienced of the two will be doing everything from picking the calling sites to actually calling the bird.

How you handle such a situation depends largely on the experience of the new hunter. If he's totally in the dark about the sport, the caller will want to leave his own gun at home and concentrate solely on helping the beginner.

In such situations I like the hunter sitting right in my lap with their back against my chest so that I can whisper directions and instructions right into the hunter's ear, and explain what is taking place during the hunt. If the hunter has some experience—that is, if he or she can tell a gobbler from a hen, knows what to listen for, and is undoubtedly safe—I usually put them at a tree up in front of me. Sometimes I may set up the hunter quite far ahead of my calling position.

You see, a turkey's hearing is so accurate that he can all but pinpoint exactly where the hen calls are coming from. If he thinks he's moving toward a hen that's fifty yards away he won't be paying as close attention to the trees that are right beside him. That takes much of the pressure off the gunner when he goes to make his move. For bowhunters, it's an unbelievable advantage.

Locating the gunner between the gobbler and the caller also gives the caller more freedom to use friction calls or to use his hands to throw calls to one side or another.

Sometimes it even pays for the caller to be up and moving when working a gobbler. If you're calling to a gobbler that's not showing a lot of movement toward the hunter, sometimes you can get his attention by backing away, but continuing to call.

Another little trick is for the caller to pull a wary, circling gobbler right past the hunter. For instance, if the gobbler is coming in from the left, I move toward the right. If he angles too far to the right, then I slip back to the left.

Running interference with other hunters is another job for a good partner. It may be as simple as standing on a country road and warning hunters wandering by, or actually stopping someone who's trying to move in and set up on your gobbling bird.

Scott Minner couldn't have been much more than eleven years old when I took him on a Missouri hunt many years ago. We'd planed the hunt for almost a year, and the hunt was all that was on Scott's mind. My plan was to make it one he'd never forget.

The hunt couldn't have begun any better. We heard a lot of gobbling at daybreak and I was able to pull two good gobblers into range, but Scott missed. He was pretty upset at first, but pulled it together later that morning as we met up with John Bostick to hunt another area. We were lucky enough to fire up another gobbler right away. At first Scott didn't even want to move in on the bird with us. He kept saying that he'd had his chance and blown it, and that now was the time for me to call one for John.

We finally talked him into moving up with us to a saddle where two ridges met. I set John up on the ridge with the gobbling turkey and sat Scott a little farther down the other ridge. As luck would have it, a bird opened up on that ridge as well.

I backtracked to the logging road that crossed the saddle, then called toward one bird and then the other. The birds were gobbling well and coming my way. My main concern was that someone else would come in on us.

Sure enough, the sounds of another caller started coming closer and closer down the old road. When the hunter walked within sight I recognized him and explained the situation. He politely sat down to listen to the action.

I kept calling as the birds became quiet. Then there was a shot from the direction of Scott. When I arrived, John was already standing beside Scott and a good gobbler. As long as I live I'll never forget what the kid said as I walked up. "I, I, I really didn't want to shoot him, Mr. Eye. I wanted John to have a chance," he said sheepishly. Then breaking into a smile he added, "but when that gobbler walked right up to twenty yards he was history!"

It's also good thing to have an extra hunter when you're blind calling and birds may come in quietly. As long as both hunters keep still, two sets of eyes can watch a lot more ground than one.

Now it is time to talk about one of the neatest, though rarely used tactics of the buddy hunting system when working a stubborn, heavily pressured gobbler.

There was one old gobbler I'd worked for several mornings that would come off a ridge gobbling but never get any closer. He'd cover a lot of ground from left to right, then back again, but he simply refused to come any closer to my calls. If I got up and moved a little closer, the turkey would head in the exact opposite direction.

I played his little game for a couple of mornings before I decided it was time to play dirty. Ron Lawson and I got to the ridge well before daylight. When I hooted, the bird gobbled. I decided to have Ron hold his ground while I circled around the ridge to the opposite side of the turkey.

Just as he had done every other morning, the bird gobbled at everything, moving from side to side but not coming any closer. And just like every other morning, when I moved a little closer the bird headed the other way.

Then I decided it was time to get even. Knowing Ron's approximate location, I gradually moved my calling sites toward the bird, almost driving him like a cow to the milk house. I'd move fifty yards closer, and his next gobble would come from fifty yards farther down the ridge. He played the game well, until he walked past the spot where Ron was waiting. There was quite a celebration when I arrived, while Ron was standing over a very old, very dead Ozark gobbler. That is certainly a hunt I will always remember.

HUNTING DAYS

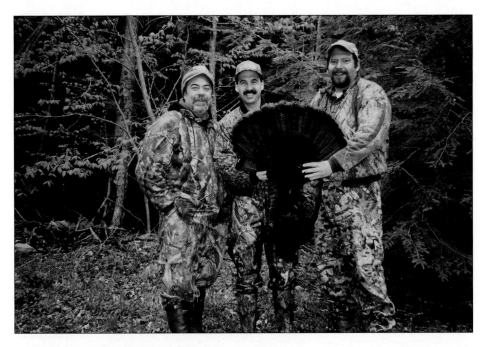

This successful New England turkey hunt is now a great memory that will last a lifetime. A small camera carried in your turkey vest will allow you to capture real emotions and the location where you took your trophy.

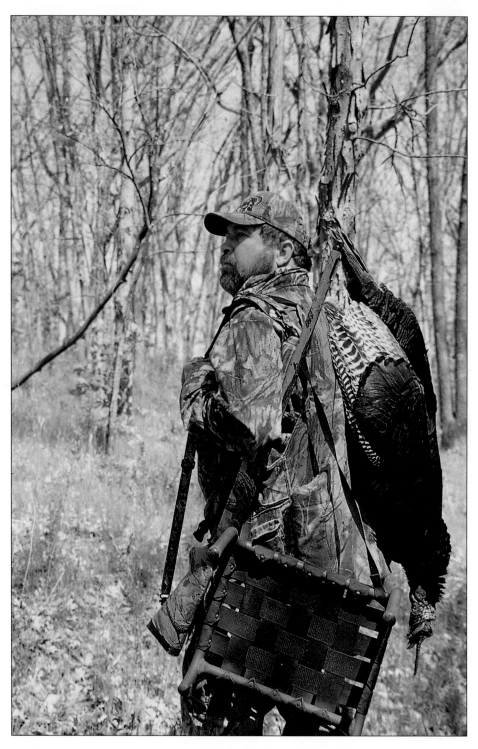

Quality accessories, a gun strap, a portable seat, good boots, and a turkey gun with an Undertaker choke tube will add to the hunter's confidence and improve the chances of success.

Steve Jones and his friend Outdoor Guide Magazine *editor Bob Whitehead with a pair of nice New Mexico Merriams.*

A small, portable ground blind works well for hunting with either gun or bow.

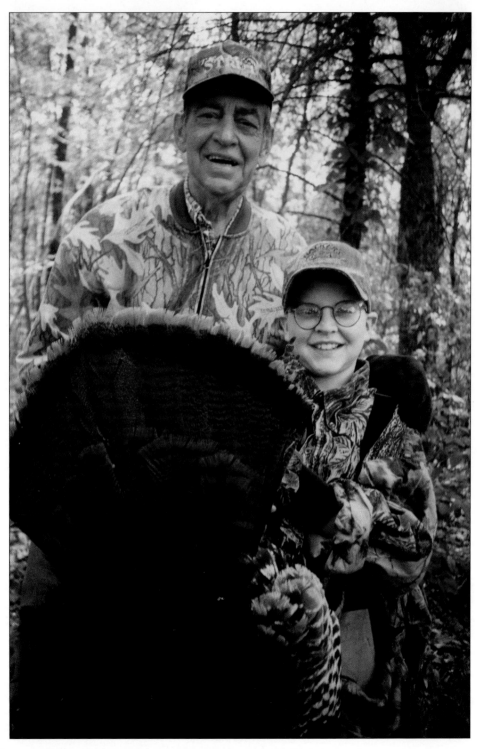

Ray Eye's dad and Ray's son David with a nice Missouri gobbler. There is always a special relationship in turkey hunting between a boy and his grandpa.

The author with two happy hunters and a pair of trophy Illinois gobblers taken the same morning.

A Hawaiian Rio Grande gobbler taken on the Big Island for a recent episode of the Cabela's Sportsman's Quest *television show.*

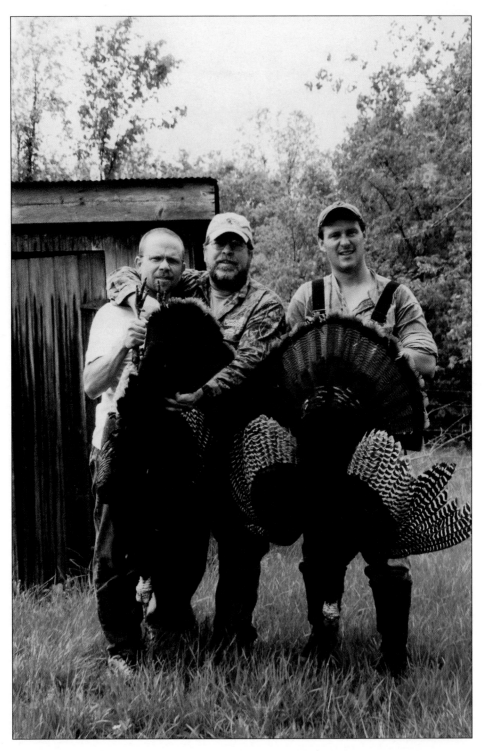

Dodd Clifton of Realtree, Ray Eye, and Jay Langston of the National Wild Turkey Federation on a Missouri turkey hunt.

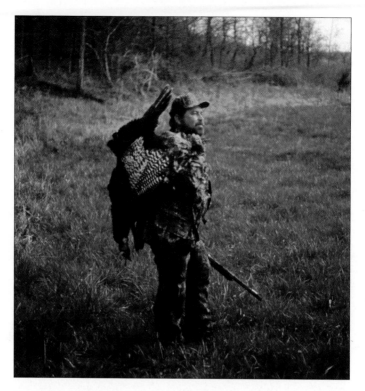

Ray Eye with a turkey that just finished its debut on a Hunter's Specialties hunting video.

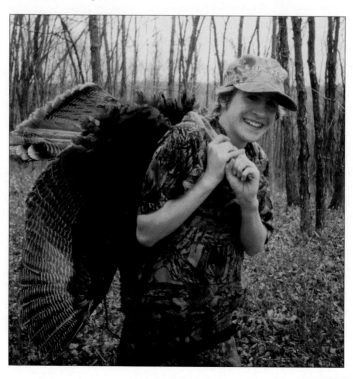

This photo says it all on this young man's first turkey hunt. Introduce youngsters to the outdoors and to turkey hunting whenever possible.

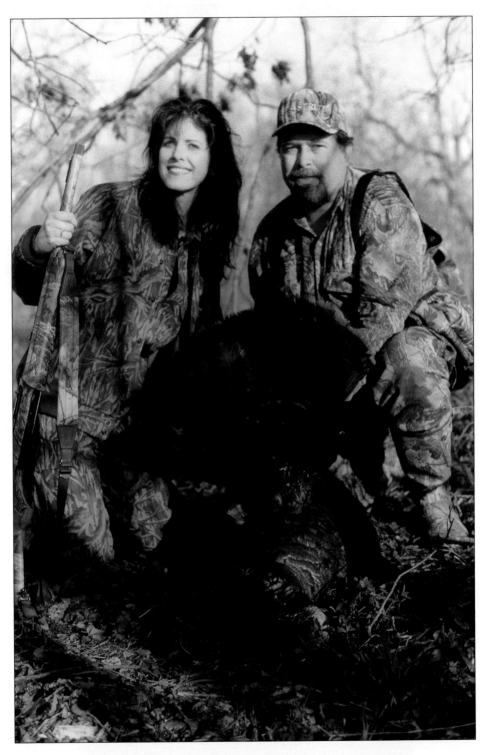

Karen Mehall of the National Rifle Association and Ray Eye, with Karen's first gobbler.

20

MAKING THE SHOT

Every hunter has been there, standing in the woods with a sick feeling as a turkey flies into the sunrise. Turkey hunters work hard all year to prepare for the hunt. Hunters pattern their guns, practice turkey calling, go over maps for days, scout for weeks, and learn the lay of the land. The season opens; they locate the bird and call him into range. Everything is good up to the final seconds, then they shoot and miss. There are many reasons why we miss. No matter how far you work a turkey, the last few yards into gun range are the most critical.

Even if you know the bird is close, it's important to keep both eyes open and your head up and off the gun stock until just before the shot for better visibility. Whatever you do, don't turn your head unless you absolutely have to. Keep your ears on full alert. Listen for the sounds of turkeys walking in the leaves and the telltale spit and drum of a strutting gobbler.

Use your eyes to scan the area in front of you. Pick the area apart bit by bit. I've called dozens of turkeys to within shooting range and found my guest unable to see them because he was either looking for the whole bird, looking too close, or looking too far.

Look for pieces of the bird: the red, white, and/or blue head of a gobbler peeking up over a log, or maybe a pair of feet on the other

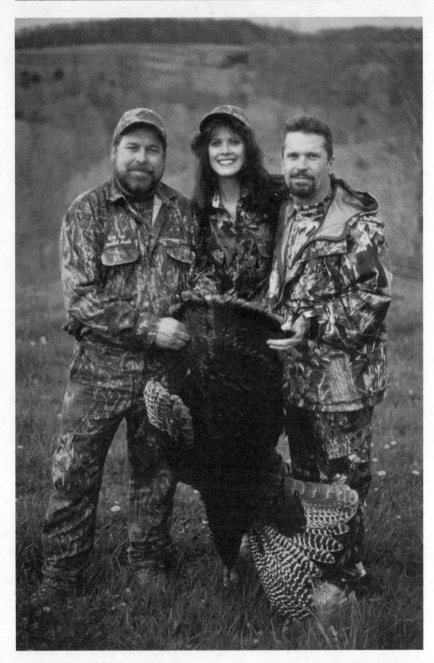

Hunting and sharing the outdoors with good friends, like Karen Mehall and Bob Walker, is much more important to me than the kill.

side of a big cedar. Don't expect the bird to be somewhere; expect him to be anywhere.

It's critical that you make absolute identification before you even think about shooting. You have to rule out every other possibility: a dog, a person, an illegal hen.

In the spring, make sure the bird's beard is visible, but don't panic once you see that it is a legal tom. If you can see him, he can see any move you make, and that means you shouldn't turn your head, move your gun, or shift your body.

Hold all movement until the bird's head is behind something like a tree or fanned tail. Regardless, make all moves slow and fluid. If you can, act only while the bird is moving, when it's the hardest for him to pinpoint anything.

Be sure the gobbler is well within your killing range and don't take any chancy shots. Be patient and your time will come.

The same goes for a bird that for some reason comes in behind you. Play the waiting game, and he'll probably come around. If he doesn't, go ahead and let him walk away. Once he's gone, adjust your position and then call him back.

I should add, though, that a good calling position will solve the problem of the bird coming in from behind. Additionally, the bird that you think is at your back may well be an entirely different bird.

Always be aware that another turkey may come in unseen and unheard. If such a bird spooks, keep your composure, because all is not lost. The putting of an alarmed bird may add more fire to the gobbler you're working. I've sometimes copied the alarm call of such a bird and the tom kept coming. Other times I've moved a small distance, sat silently for twenty to thirty minutes, and restarted the gobbler.

Never, never shoot a turkey when he is in strut and his head is all pulled back into his body: a shot at such a small area could mean a wounded turkey. Wait. He'll stick his head up to look for the hen. If

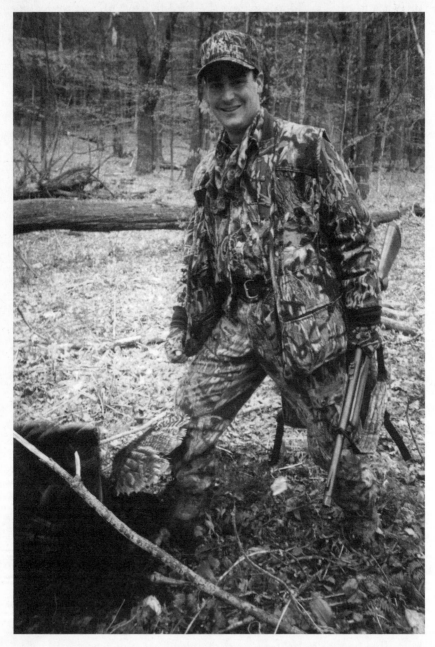

Call the turkey in close, and make a good shot. Do not jump up and run with a loaded gun. Put your foot on the tom's neck and hold it to the ground.

he doesn't, give a sharp putt. If you're not using a diaphragm call, just do the best you can with your lips. Either way, he'll raise his head like a periscope to see what's going on, exposing all of his head and neck.

If you have a loud safety on your gun, use one finger on each side of the button to slowly slide it through quietly. If your gun has a hammer, hold the trigger until the hammer has eased back into its locked position.

Be sure that your head is down on the gun and your cheek is where it should he, and that you're aiming the shotgun as if it were a rifle. Aim for the turkey's cherry-sized wattles and squeeze the trigger.

If the gobbler's within gun range and your gun is shooting as it should, the bird will be yours.

Don't run to the down bird. Running through the woods with a loaded gun is an accident waiting to happen, even if the bird is only twenty yards away. Sure, you don't want to waste any time, but just get up and watch the bird, and make sure you have an open shot if the bird tries to get back up. If the tom's head is up, shoot him again. There's nothing wrong with an insurance shot, but be careful where you place it. I talked with a hunter who called a bird up and shot it, When his partner ran up to within five yards of the gobbler, it started the usual flopping, and the youngster unloaded his three-inch 12-gauge right into the bird's body.

If the bird is still flopping, put your foot on his neck until he stops. Sometimes the shock to his nervous system may keep him bouncing for a while. Never pick up a bird before he's totally life-less. Darned near every turkey hunter I know has gotten excited and grabbed a big tom by his legs, only to be cut deep by the bird's spurs. Others have had less painful but equally interesting encounters.

John Hauer tells about guiding a pair of hunters on his ranch in South Dakota's Black Hills. It was one of those mornings when everything seemed to be going right. John brought a jake up at first light, and one of the hunters dropped it like a rock.

Wanting to get the other hunter a bird while they were still gobbling, Hauer rushed out to the jake, looked it over, and stuffed in his back pouch. A little later that morning Hauer was working another hot bird when all hell broke loose.

The flopping of the bird in his pouch almost knocked him over. When the jake broke free of the pouch, his head was up and his feet were moving. Hauer made a grab for the bird's neck, which started a wrestling match that the guide barely won, and not without a good flogging. He finally did get the second bird into range only to have his hunter miss it clean. Some days are shineola and some days are. . .

21

AUTUMN TURKEYS

Fall turkey season: the beautiful fall colors, the frosty mornings, and the unmistakable sounds of wild turkeys waking on the roost to welcome a new day. The sights, the sounds, calling to a flock of birds, listening to the crunching in the frosty leaves as twenty-plus birds run toward you. I have hunted fall turkey for almost thirty years and yes, I enjoy each and every season even more than the one before.

I hope by sharing and passing on to you my experiences from the fall turkey woods, if you have not tried fall hunting, you will. Fall hunting will make you a better caller and turkey hunter, and just maybe make it really difficult for you to decide which you enjoy more, spring or fall. One thing is certain for me: Hunting fall gobblers is my passion; there is nothing in turkey hunting I enjoy more. Bow, muzzleloader, or shotgun, it really does not matter. I remember many hunts throughout the years, but this one just happens to come to mind.

During the early to mid-1980s I left my Ozark hills to try fall hunting in north Missouri. After entering the woods, Clinton Steele and I had split up to work opposite sides of a river that divided his property.

Total darkness turned to full light without a sound and with no sight of the four longbeards we'd seen the previous day. I started with soft gobbler yelps at first light. Now, close to an hour later, I'd built to an aggressive series of calls with fifteen to twenty yelps.

Sitting with my back against an old tree at the edge of a logging road, I was sending calls alternately to the left and to the right. My confidence with the spot had all but disappeared when I sent one more set of yelps to the left. That's when I first saw them, the four large birds trotting across a clearing a hundred yards away.

By the time I slid around to face them I could hear the gobblers cutting as they closed the distance. I let loose some aggressive cutting and gobbler yelping. One of the toms stood erect, flapped his wings, and quickened his pace.

The toms were gradually skirting to my left when they came into gun range. The first of the flock trotted right past me, and the next two were a little too far to the left. The back bird was at the fringe of gun range and coming right at me. I pointed my gun slowly and hoped he'd keep coming.

Out of the corner of my eye I could see two of the toms pacing back and forth. They called from time to time as they searched for the source of the calls they'd followed. The problem was the lead bird. He had looped in behind me, and I could hear him walking closer and closer. By that time I had stopped calling and was just trying to hold as still as the tree that was supporting my awkward slouch.

The crunching in the leaves grew louder and louder until I was sure the gobbler could be no more than a few feet away. Finally sensing something was wrong, he took off running and putting. Hearing the commotion, the bird in front of me raised his head at twenty-eight steps. I pulled the trigger when the bead of my Remington settled on his neck. The 20½-pound tom folded at the shot.

I moved up quickly and admired the bird and his 10-inch beard. But it was quite a while before my nerves were calmed enough to head for the truck.

I remember wondering how anyone could not call such a hunt exciting and rank it right up with the best of spring memories.

Maybe the reason some people don't get too fired up about fall hunting is because they simply don't understand it very well. Many states started their spring seasons years before their fall seasons, which meant hunters learned first of gobbling birds and hen calling.

Actually the fall hunt is turkey hunting for real turkeys. Their actions and behavior are typical for three hundred days a year. Behavior in the mating season is the exception. Yet a hunter steps into the fall woods, makes a few seductive yelps, wonders why he doesn't get a gobble, and consequently concludes that fall is a second-rate season.

The key to having fun in the fall is understanding the turkeys and what they're doing. This is often a time of flocks that range from two to two dozen or more turkeys. Understanding and knowing how to take advantage of the bird's gregarious nature is the first step to success.

During a year that has a good hatch, many of the flocks are made up of hens with poults. Sometimes there is only one hen and her brood, but there may be up to four or five mature hens with a mob of poults milling around.

Still caught between adolescence and adulthood, groups of jakes often band together and wander the woods. Again, they can number anywhere from a pair to a dozen or more shortbeards in one bunch. Barren hens (those that didn't raise a brood) will often band together in a similar manner.

Then there are the old longbeards. Occasionally an old patriarch is off by himself, but more often a mature tom accompanies a bachelor flock of similar birds.

But always keep in mind that there are no absolutes in turkey hunting, especially in fall flocks. Almost any combination is possible. I've seen longbeards with hens and poults. You're liable to see a jake running with anything that will tolerate it. Late in the fall it's not uncommon to see turkeys of all ages and both sexes in one huge flock, especially on a winter food source.

The important idea to remember is that each bird out there has its place in the pecking order. Even late-hatched poults no bigger than barnyard chickens have their dominant bird. Turkeys relate to pecking order every week of the year. The hunter who knows how to use that fact to his advantage can have a great hunt in the fall.

You see, in the spring you usually call from one sex to the other, but in the fall you often call from like bird to like bird, such as from poult to poult or old tom to old tom. (One exception is calling like a hen to regroup a scattered brood.) All, and I mean all, types of birds can be called in the fall if you simply speak their language. But first you have to find a bird to talk to.

Scouting is as important in the fall as it is in the spring. In fact, getting out and walking the woods is imperative because usually there will be no booming gobbles that can be heard for long distances.

With a fresh crop of leaves and mast on the ground, any scratchings should be easy to see. You should also keep an eye out for the usual droppings, tracks, and feathers. In traditional hardwood forests, check oak groves for evidence of feeding flocks. If there's a lot of agriculture and little mast, check places like corn and soybean fields. Fall turkeys will normally be found wherever the food is.

Be sure to keep your ears open whenever you're scouting in the woods. Listen for the sounds of calling hens or the wingbeats of a flock flying up or down from a roost.

In some parts of the country it's possible to do some scouting with binoculars, looking for birds that are feeding in the open. Since fall birds sometimes have very regular behavior patterns, talking with deer or squirrel hunters or local farmers can often put you in the right area.

As in the spring, some of your best prospects are birds on the roost. If you've done your homework you may already know the general location of a roosted flock.

If you're starting from scratch, get to high ground and listen carefully for turkey talk. Most people are surprised at the amount of yelping, purring, and other conversation at a fall roost. If you don't hear anything from your post, try a few kee-kee runs. There aren't many hens in the woods that can resist the pleading calls of a lost poult, especially when they're on the roost.

The basic approach for working a fall roost is the same as for the spring. Get as close to the birds as possible and try to be situated where the turkeys will want to land.

If you listen well, you should be able to tell which bird is doing the most calling. You should then call directly to that bird, remembering to call from like bird to like bird.

Do whatever that turkey is doing, but with a little more intensity. If it yelps three times, you yelp five times. If it starts cutting, you cut right back. Chances are the excitement will get the other birds calling too. When that happens you're in for a lot of fun.

Over the years, including back before Missouri had a fall season, when I called to learn more and to take photos, I'll bet I've worked several hundred groups of birds on the roost, ranging from a single bird to a flock of close to forty. One particular hunt comes to mind.

A hen had cut my kee-kee whistles just down the ridge from where my client and I were waiting. Moving quickly, we set up slightly above the bird, about seventy yards away.

As it began to get light, what sounded like the same hen started with some soft talk, and I joined the conversation. In the space of a few minutes we went from soft purrs and clucks to aggressive cutting.

Soon it sounded as if the treetops in front of us were filled with excited turkeys.

When it got light enough to see well, I let out one more aggressive string of calls. The sound of beating wings literally filled our ears. The turkeys hit the ground calling excitedly, and we could hear them moving about to regroup.

I gave the birds a few minutes to get together and quiet down while my client got his gun up on his knee and settled into a comfortable position.

The woods grew still when I let out some soft purrs. All hell broke loose when I followed with some aggressive yelps, then cutting. The flock literally charged up the hill, the dominant hen in the lead cutting nonstop while the other birds sounded intermittent, excited calls.

Within seconds the whole mob was milling about in front of us. My client wisely took a young gobbler standing off to the side of the main bunch.

FLOCK CALLING

The traditional method of calling fall turkeys advocates walking the soles off your boots until you find a flock, then scattering the flock to the four corners of the earth. Yes, it is method with a history of some success, and I enjoy a good vocal recall as much as anyone.

However, turkeys don't always have to be scattered to be called. They're pretty social, and because of the pecking order, they'll more than likely want to investigate any new turkey, a new voice that they hear. Again, the hardest part is often finding the turkeys to call. Besides, after walking for miles in the Ozarks, finally finding a flock of birds, it did not make much sense to me to run them all off, especially when I could have called them to me in the first place.

I like to move and call much as I do in the spring. I'll pick an area that scouting has shown to have a good population, then work

The fall classic. Turkey hunting's greatest trophy is the fall gobbler. This turkey was called in off the roost and taken by "Doctor Doom."

the ridges, setting up every few hundred yards or as far away as my last calls may have carried.

The basics are the same: try to set up where your calls can be heard simultaneously in several good areas. Get comfortable and let the woods settle down before you start calling. Start off with soft and short calls in case there's a flock just over the ridge. As time progresses, make your calls more aggressive.

Remember that in the fall the sexy mating yelps might not do much good. If you're in a state that allows fall hunters to take any sex, to call hens or young birds, you use a lot of kee-kee whistles until you get an old hen to answer. Then imitate her response.

Any of the turkey calling devices will work in the fall. A good slate call that can produce deep purrs and aggressive putts and yelps can work well, as can a box call. If you're going to use a mouth call, stick with something that's got a little raspy sound to it, like a call with a split reed, like the 2.5. At least it works well for me.

As in the spring, you can expect each turkey to respond to calls in different ways. Some open up and come in screaming like kamikazes. Others take their time and come in without muttering a sound.

Really use your ears. Many hunters, conditioned to the booming gobbles of spring, have problems hearing some of the soft purrs and putts of a fall bird. Listen for the sounds of turkeys walking in the dry leaves.

Since they're coming for reasons other than sex, fall turkeys may or may not be a little slower to respond than spring birds. If you have some confidence in your location, and if you know there are turkeys in the area, be prepared to wait forty-five minutes to an hour. Always scan the area thoroughly before getting up quietly and slowly to move to your next calling station.

As with all turkey hunts, keep your eyes and ears open when trying to locate a fall flock. Sometimes you'll get a response but the birds won't come in. There could be a barrier between you and the birds that they don't want to cross, or perhaps the birds' daily routine takes them in the other direction. Either way, by changing calling locations, you may get them to come right in.

If the turkeys are in traditional hardwoods feeding on nuts you can often literally track them down. A few years ago a friend and I were working a big tract of national forest, but were coming up with a whole lot of nothing before we happened upon some fairly fresh turkey scratchings near an old logging road.

Figuring the direction of the flock, we worked our way down the logging road, stopping to set up where we could send calls to both sides of the road.

Our first few calling sites brought no answers to my calls, but we noticed that the scratchings were beginning to look much fresher. Our fourth setup was at the junction of the logging road and another road. I made a soft call and a turkey answered from what sounded like fifty yards in front of us. I cut and yelped back at the bird, and the entire flock of about twenty-five turned and came running. My partner took a young bird at about ten feet.

There are times, such as when you're in an area that you haven't scouted well, when trying to find a flock of turkeys to work is frustrating. Often all the birds for a mile or more around may congregate in one area of a certain field or grove of oaks.

All you can do is keep moving and calling until you either strike birds or run out of daylight. But don't give up. The turkeys have to be somewhere, and if they're all in one spot the hunt can really get exciting.

Mark Lowder and I once moved and called all day to hear but a few distant hen yelps. Right before dark we decided to try one last spot. I cut a few times, then yelped, and a turkey gobbled at us. (Yes, turkeys gobble year round, and you will hear gobbles in the fall.)

I cut back a reply, and we heard the bird cutting and moving closer. The next time I called, flocks of turkeys opened up on each side of us and started coming in. There were turkeys of all sizes coming in from three directions. Mark took a nice eastern.

SCATTER AND RECALL

Even though scattering a flock is not my first-choice method, it's a technique that can't be overlooked. I've used the scatter method when a shot has been missed, when the birds hang up just out of range, the birds make us, or when I hear another hunter coming into my location.

The key to a good scatter is to get the birds to go in as many different directions as possible. To do that you really have to surprise them. I've heard some hunters talk about running at a flock while firing their guns. That sounds unsafe to me, and if you're that close, why not just shoot a bird?

It's far safer, and just as effective, to lay your gun carefully down, then rush the flock barking like a dog, clapping your hands, or making some other commotion. Try to get as close to the center of the flock as possible and watch to see the direction of flight.

If you're working a group of hens and poults, the easiest tactic is to set up at the scatter point. If you think you can get between some of the birds and the scatter point without spooking them, it might be worth a try. The closer you can get, the less can go wrong.

I usually don't call until the turkeys begin to regroup. Sometimes the scattered birds will start calling to regroup within a couple of minutes, but sometimes they don't call for an hour. If the woods are fairly open and they can see well, they may regroup by sight and you'll be out of luck. It's even more disheartening when a scattered flock flies to open pastures.

Once you get a bird to call you can usually imitate him, only make the sound more pleading. If you're working young birds you can do well with the kee-kee, and you can often get by just whistling it. If you want to use hen yelps, try a long, lingering, lost call of twenty to thirty yelps.

And speaking of hens, I often ask the people who hunt with me not to shoot the brood hen, so that she can help the brood until spring. She may even pull off another clutch. Then again, I don't want that same hen calling all the poults away from me. If she were to show up again I'd run out and spook her off.

For any number of reasons, a hunter may want to keep scattering a flock. One time a friend and I worked a big mixed flock into bow range and each took three shots. Then we rushed out to flush the birds and retrieve our arrows.

We set back up, waited a while, then called some of the birds back in. This time we shot all of our arrows and flushed the birds again. This went on for the better part of the afternoon until we were totally out of arrows. I did manage to hit a couple of pretty nice trees, and my buddy brought back some feathers from the racing stripe that he shaved across the back of a young gobbler.

There have also been times when I've scattered a flock, then gone to get a friend or another client so he could fill a tag as well. Remember the flock of twenty-five that I tracked and then called in? I brought two more friends to the place where we'd killed the young tom and called in a scattered bird for each of them.

But always remember that scattering a flock of turkeys can lead to an uncertain situation. I've pulled off perfect scatters at first light, then never heard a peep from the birds. I've also rushed in, only to have the entire flock flush and head in the same direction.

Without a doubt the best and most successful scattering occurs when you can scare a flock off a roost late in the evening. You can often get close and send them in all different directions. After spending a night by itself on a limb, most turkeys will be more than anxious to regroup at first light.

A few years ago a friend came over to Missouri for two and a half days of fall hunting. We spent the first two days concentrating on longbeards, working several birds but always encountering one small mishap or another.

As we returned to the house that second evening, my brother Marty was just getting back from a hunt. He'd played with a mixed flock for an hour or more, passing up a bunch of shots at hens and young birds but not quite getting the one longbeard within range.

Knowing that Mike we would be hunting the next morning, he listened for the flock to fly up to roost, then scattered them. Back at the house he described where the birds had been roosted and where they'd flown so that we could go back the next morning.

The scheme worked like a charm. We slipped to the scatter point just before first light, and the turkeys were already calling. Soon it sounded as if we were set up in the middle of a turkey farm. There were purrs, clucks, yelps, cuts, and even an occasional adolescent gobble sounding from all around us.

All it took was a little lost-hen calling. The birds started flying down all around us. More excited hen calls with a few kee-kees tossed in had the birds calling and coming from all directions.

My friend had set his mind on taking the first turkey that came by. He dropped a young bird coming in with a mature hen. He didn't know it, but the longbeard wasn't far behind.

FALL GOBBLERS

I've saved the best of the fall season for last: hunting fall gobblers. For years I heard people claim that hunters had to ambush or simply luck onto an autumn longbeard. Some hunters said it was impossible to call in gobblers that were lacking the passion of the mating season.

I entered the fall turkey woods early one October morning many years ago. I headed to a place where I'd scouted a nice bachelor flock of longbeards. Like clockwork, at the first hints of daylight I heard the birds' soft talk from a roost near the edge of a big Ozark hollow.

I set up and waited a few minutes before calling to them. They answered back with some yelps and cuts, and I called again. The birds flew down to my right and started excited clucking as soon as their feet hit the leaves. One series of aggressive gobbler yelps had them on their way.

Resting on one knee with big hickories at my front and rear, I faced a large blowdown about ten yards in front of me and a slight break in the hill an equal distance beyond that. I could occasionally glimpse the tops of the toms' heads as they came. I could hear their yelps and cuts almost nonstop. I matched them call for call until they were just beyond the break, when I shut up and got ready.

The birds purred and clucked as they moved up an old trail that passed in front of the blowdown. I drew my bow when all three toms were behind the brush, and released an arrow into the tom that walked into the clear first. He weighed twenty pounds and had a ten-inch beard.

There are no real secrets to calling fall gobblers. The basics are the same as calling young birds or hens. Call gobbler to gobbler and try to break into the existing pecking order as the cocky new kid on the block.

Get a bird to respond, imitate his calls with a little more intensity to get him fired up, and you may see things some turkey hunters never expect to see in the fall. I've heard some excited turkeys gobble once, and others gobble every step of the way, just as they do in spring.

It's even more common to see toms strutting as they broadcast their roles in the pecking order. Over the years I've seen fall turkeys get so excited that they break into a fight.

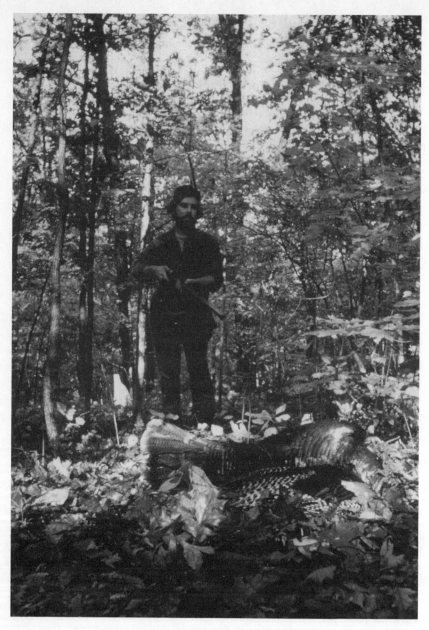

The author has taken fall gobblers with a muzzleloader for many years. Radiotelemetry studies, check station data, and extensive research indicate that hunters harvest less than 4% of fall turkey populations. This research shows that fall hunting does not adversely impact the flock or reduce the quality of spring hunting.

During the fall hunt, hunters call "bird to bird" to call hens, sound like a hen to call gobblers, or call like a gobbler. Wild turkeys can be very vocal in the fall.

On the traditional fall hunt, hunters find and scatter hens and young turkeys. During the flock "recall" hunters use the kee-kee, yelps, and clucks. During most states' fall turkey seasons, either sex is legal.

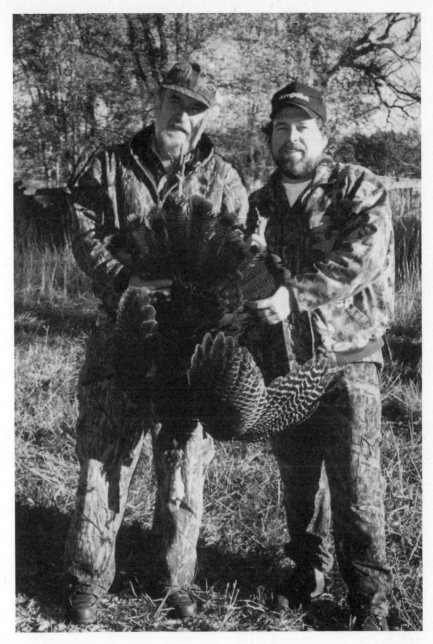

Regardless whether you hunt young turkeys, jakes, or gobblers, fall hunting is about the experience. It's a great time to be in the woods. Hunters will learn more about calling and wild turkey vocalizations than at any other time of the year.

Fall turkey hunting is widely misunderstood. Yes, hunters can call fall turkeys. Gobblers will gobble and display. Strutting, dominant gobblers are fairly common because of the pecking order.

Marty Eye with a fall longbeard called with gobbler yelping.

From left to right, Bob Whitehead, Ray Eye, and Marty Eye with Bob's first fall gobbler.

Remember that gobblers sometimes call with a little slower rhythm and deeper tone than hens. It depends on the excitement level; there are times an excited tom yelping is difficult to tell from a hen yelping. If you like a mouth call, try something raspy like a split reed or a 2.5 cutter-type diaphragm.

As you've already read, working gobblers on the roost can be extremely effective, but you can also do well by moving and calling. I seldom intentionally scatter a bachelor flock of fall gobblers. When I do scatter toms for whatever reason, I've often had pretty good success getting them to recall and regroup.

Even when you prefer a big bird, don't pass up the chance to work any bird that will answer a call. It's not uncommon to happen upon a mixed flock that has a longbeard or two in its midst.

You can use hens and poults to your advantage in getting a gobbler flock to respond. Several times I've been playing with a hen and her brood, getting them all fired up, and a gobbler flock has come running in to see what all the commotion is about.

The most important tools are confidence and patience. You don't need to be a pro. Over the years I've talked a lot of doubters into trying fall hunts, and quite a few of them have called in and scored on a gobbler during their first season. For some, success came remarkably quickly.

The first time Mike Pearce and I fall-hunted together I did all of the calling all morning, but we split to cover more ground that afternoon. Just before we parted, I showed Mike a few important calls and sent him down a promising ridge.

At his first calling site, a bird answered Mike with a few soft yelps. Mike yelped back with a little more feeling. A little later the bird yelped back, and the conversation continued until the long-beard was within twenty feet.

Even if it takes you some time to call in a fall gobbler, stick with it. Sooner or later you'll be sitting in the frosty, full-colored woods with your heart in your throat as you watch a gobbler flock so excited that the birds are shoving each other back and forth as they come.

Experience it once and you'll be hooked for life. That's one of turkey hunting's few certainties.

22

BOWHUNTING–THE ULTIMATE CHALLENGE

Bowhunting the wild turkey is without a doubt the ultimate challenge in turkey hunting. Whether you bowhunt the spring season or fall, calling and hunting tactics for either season are pretty much the same as when using a gun. But the end result usually is not. After my first bowhunt for turkeys back in 1975, I was hooked for life, and today I would rather hunt fall gobblers with a bow than anything else.

As I think back over the years, I could tell hundreds of stories about bowhunting turkey, but one in particular comes to mind. It was late fall, early winter, and a huge flock of turkeys had already settled into their winter pattern. A mixed flock of about forty poults, hens, jakes, and some adult gobblers was roosting at the top of a long, wide Ozark hollow night after night.

Shortly after sunrise they'd fly down, head down the hollow, and cross a little stream to feed in a cut bean field. My brother Marty and I had set up about fifty yards apart halfway down the hollow that morning.

The birds woke up talking, and we helped to fuel their fire with our own yelps and excited cutting. For a while they pitched from the

Hunting wild turkeys in spring or fall with a bow, gun, or muzzleloader requires the same tactics and calling skills.

trees a bird or two at a time. The last half of the flock left as one, filling the air with the sound of wingbeats and excited calls.

Marty poured it on the birds while I sat back and listened. Marty was set up and calling from an old, blown-down cedar, and the birds were answering nonstop.

You didn't have to be an experienced turkey hunter to know that turkeys were closing in on Marty's location. Their calls echoed through the hollow, as did the sound of close to eighty feet hustling through the carpet of brittle leaves. The suspense kept building and building. I could tell that the turkeys were literally swarming all around Marty, yelping, cutting, clucking, and even occasionally gobbling.

Then came much different sounds: twang, ping, ping, bang, ping, *whack*, followed by even more excited turkey calls. Then twang, ping, ping, bang, ping, *whack!* Next came the roar of wingbeats. Seconds after they faded, the sound of profanity came from Marty's cedar.

When I walked over I found Marty, knife in hand, trying to cut a broadhead out of an old oak and muttering some unkind words about turkeys. The flock had surrounded him, from poults on up to old gobblers. During the gun season one of the big old boys would have been flopping in the leaves. Since it was bow season all Marty had was a couple of "almosts," one very nice oak, and an unforgettable memory.

So it goes with bowhunting for turkeys.

Each year more and more states offer hunters special archery turkey seasons. Most take place in the fall and run for several weeks, sometimes as long as three months. The bowhunter can take any bird.

There can also be some good bowhunting during the spring season. The spring seasons aren't usually as lengthy and are for gobblers only, but they do have their advantages. For one thing there is usually more foliage in spring to help the hunter get a shot. And then the birds themselves are strutting, gobbling, and carrying on. If you think the hunt is exciting with a gun you should to try it with a bow.

A hunter who knows what he's doing can squeeze in a lot of fun during the spring and fall seasons. With much skill and an equal amount of luck he may carry home one of the most coveted prizes in bowhunting.

The first thing a new bowhunter has to realize is the difference between gun and bowhunting. Getting the bird up close is the toughest part when you're hunting with a scattergun. It's just half of the battle when you're using a couple of sticks and a string.

You simply can't get good shots off at every bird that comes into range; so you need lots of chances. That's why I suggest most newcomers to the sport look to the fall season—the later the better.

In most areas you'll find turkeys concentrated at one major food source, following somewhat regular patterns. They'll usually roost in one general area and follow the same basic path to food day after day. The birds respond well to calls. You'll usually see several once you find their wintering grounds.

Late fall is the author's favorite time to bowhunt gobblers.

Once you're familiar with their pattern it's time to start looking for a good calling site within their territory. The hardest part of getting a bowshot at a turkey is simply drawing your bow. Unless everything is just right, they see the motion and spook.

A good blind is very effective to hide movement. Natural, portable, or permanent blinds are all good choices. Hunters should select a blind that works best for them and the area they are hunting. The new pop-up camo blinds are very effective, easy to move and set up, and very easy to shoot out of. A decoy setup will help draw the birds to the blind, and will take the turkeys' attention off the blind and hunter.

My favorite method of bowhunting turkeys is moving and calling, hunting aggressively until I find the birds. On a bird's approach I use the terrain to mask the movement of my draw. For instance, as when gun hunting, I set up with a ridge or break a short distance in front of me. But I also like to have a blowdown, brush pile, or some big cedars between me and the break in the hill.

Marty Eye with a turkey taken from a ground blind. Archery equipment that is used for white-tailed deer is adequate for turkeys.

With either a compound or a recurve bow, practice is absolutely vital, because accuracy is everything.

Common sense says that you never draw on a wild turkey when you can see his head and neck, because he'll see you and spook. I wait until he's behind that blowdown or big cedar in front of me, then make my move just before he steps back out into the open.

Shooting from a sitting position was always difficult with a bow. I would rest my old recurve bow vertically in front of me on one knee. I consider the tree in front of me more important than the tree at my back. By leaning a bit I can use this tree to block me from the bird's sight. Another tree close behind me, to break my outline, would be additional insurance.

One of the most important elements in taking a wild turkey with a bow is learning when to make your move, then making it quickly. Personally, for years I shot instinctively with my recurve bow, which didn't take long. If you shoot a bow with sights, practice coming to full draw and releasing in one fluid motion. Bows are much better today; these new high-tech compounds are very fast

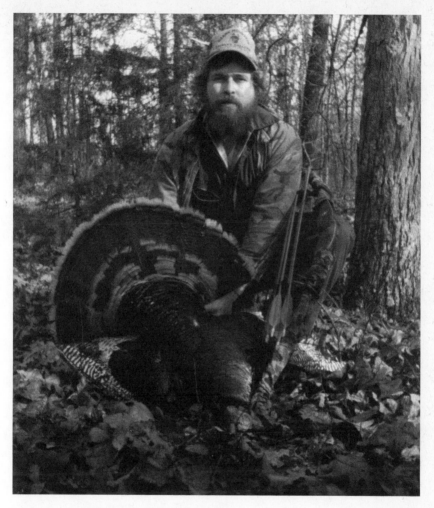

Ray Eye in the Missouri Ozarks in the early 1980s.

and accurate. Some have as much as seventy percent let-off, so you can hold at full draw forever. Most are short enough that you can sit on the ground and shoot. Technology has definitely improved the odds of taking a turkey with a bow.

Putting the shot where it needs to go is always a challenge. Turkeys have a habit of taking an extra step about the time the bow-string slips from your fingers. Even when they're standing stone still

Ray Eye with his first fall gobbler with a bow, 1975.

you have to hit them in the right place. The closer they are, the easier that is. I never shoot at a turkey with a bow if he's over twenty-five yards away, and I prefer them at twenty feet.

As with white-tailed deer, I try to put my arrow right into the vitals. The turkey facing away from me offers my favorite shot because everything is so easy to see. Put an arrow through the upper part of the bird's back and you've struck home, through the goodies. The result is a bird down that goes nowhere; most just thrash a little and it is over very quickly.

A bird that's walking straight at you offers a good shot as well. If it's a gobbler, try to put the arrow right where the beard enters the body. If it's a hen or a poult, improvise. Be sure you keep your shots high and forward if the bird is standing sideways.

There seem to be many theories about what makes the best turkey-hunting arrow. I shoot the same thing I use for deer: a big three- or four-blade, very sharp broadhead. Its cutting edge is wide and puts it right where it must be, in the vitals. Why would you shoot anything different than you would to take any big game animal? I'm convinced that accuracy, good shot selection, close range, and blowing a huge hole through the vitals is the key.

I talk to thousands of hunters each year at outdoor shows, and stories of birds running or flying away after a shot with a bow usually are the main topic of discussion.

During those conversations I usually discover that many of those birds were hit improperly, many at long, long ranges. You must be very patient and very selective of the shot you take. Keep your shots in as close as possible for better accuracy and also for quicker access to the downed bird after the shot.

There are no set rules for what to do after you shoot a turkey with an arrow. If the bird is close and flopping hard, I rush him, put my foot on his neck, and then wait until he stops thrashing.

Play it by ear. If you hit a bird and he jumps up and starts running you have to decide if you can get to him or if doing so would just spook him even more. You also have to consider how safe it is to go running through the woods after a turkey that may have a razor-sharp broadhead sticking out of his body.

If you have a string-tracker, make sure the line is flowing smoothly and let it do the work. If you don't have a string-tracker, use your eyes and ears to figure out where the wounded bird is headed.

As with deer, don't be in a big hurry to find a wounded turkey that's run off. Check the ground for tiny drops of blood and a trail of feathers. There usually won't be much to follow, so pay close attention.

If the bird's hit hard, it will probably head downhill and might well try to hole up in the thickest cover around. Check deep within brush piles, blowdowns, undercut banks, and the like. Make a thorough search for a well-shot turkey and you'll probably find it.

But more than likely, finding errant arrows will consume more of your time than looking for hit turkeys. You'll also spend more time talking about the shots that you *almost* had instead of the ones you had. There are a seemingly infinite number of things that can go wrong when you're bowhunting for turkeys. Even the most well-planned hunts can fall to pieces in a hurry. Then again, sooner or later the odds will change.

The hunt with my two friends was an impulsive idea. I wasn't really ready when they showed up, and I wasn't as prepared as I like to be when we walked into the woods.

After a while we split up to cover three separate ridges. We hadn't been apart long when a bird yelped a response to my calls. The bird was close, just over the lip of a ridge. It couldn't have been sixty yards away.

As luck would have it, I was set up in a perfect calling site with a little ravine in front of me and a scattering of cedars all around. I let out a few more fall calls that were met by excited clucks. Countering with some cutting, I could hear the birds moving my way.

My heart went into overdrive when five longbeards came trotting over the ridge in a tight little group. They never broke stride as they dropped down into the ravine.

When they were all out of sight I raised my bow and got it to full draw just as the lead bird stepped up into sight. With his head and neck behind a cedar and the rest of his body totally exposed, he stopped, barely fifteen feet away. The arrow seemed to release itself and smacked the bird right where it was supposed to.

The time between when I first heard the toms to when I stood over one couldn't have been more than a couple of minutes. It was my best bird with a bow: 22½ pounds, long spurs, and a bushy 11-inch beard.

I know I may never bow-kill another bird in the Ozarks to top that one. But I'll keep trying, and I'll keep missing shots and spooking turkeys when I'm trying to draw. It will still be lots of fun, and after all, fun is what turkey hunting is all about. The kill, especially the killing of a trophy bird, is just a bonus.

23

GEAR AND ACCESSORIES

You just pulled into your favorite turkey place in the early morning darkness. After fumbling for your flashlight, you check your turkey vest and make sure you have everything you need for your hunt. Turkey calls, sandpaper, ammunition, bug spray, bottled water, strut seat, head net, gloves, and of course your turkey gun. You make your way down the old logging road to a familiar place on the ridge.

As the world wakes up with the first orange streaks in the sky, you pull your owl call from your vest and really break the silence. The response from the tom's roost is exactly what you had hoped for. After taking a few seconds to pore over your mental map of the area, you walk quickly about two hundred yards and then head right to a little clearing on the tom's level. There are no obstacles between the gobbler and you, only open woods and the remnants of an old two-track road.

With a slight drop in the ridge thirty yards in front of you, you nestle into the base of a big oak, drop a head net over your face, rest the gun on your knees, and then yelp aggressively. A booming gobble is the immediate response from down below. The bird, possibly a veteran of four or five spring seasons, has showed some hesitation, but well-timed cutting has brought him to just beyond the rise. He's close enough that you can easily hear him spitting and drumming. The last gobble is loud enough that you actually feel it. You give a couple of soft yelps and you can see just the top of a fanned tail moving slowly toward you.

Seconds later the entire bird is in sight, almost glowing in the early morning light. For an instant or two you're almost spellbound by the bird's beauty and size. Another thundering gobble snaps you back to reality. You encircle the trigger of your shotgun with a quivering finger and start to pull.

The real work—getting a mature gobbler to come that close— is behind you. The hunt is already an overwhelming success, but what happens next will determine whether the tom will become the icing on an already unforgettable cake. The concept is very simple: You need something that will travel from you to the turkey with enough shock to turn off his central nervous system. That's not too difficult with the right kind of gun and ammunition.

TURKEY GUNS

As you have already read, I shot my first turkey with an old Winchester Model 97 12-gauge pump gun. If you'd asked me then, I'd have sworn that such a gun was the best, if the not the only, gun for turkey hunting.

Since then I've seen gobblers shot with $20,000 custom guns and with old hand-me-downs held together simply by a combination of rust, electrician's tape, and a pair of strong hands. I'm convinced there is no one shotgun that does the best job of killing a turkey. There are an abundance of guns that will do the job. You have to decide which is right for you and is adequate for the area and terrain you are hunting

For the past ten to fifteen years the trend has been toward bigger when it comes to turkey guns. There's no doubt that a big 10-gauge or a 12-gauge full of three-inch magnums can make a heck of a turkey gun, but this tendency can be taken a little too far. Do not get a big gun because you want to shoot farther.

Back in the 1970s a few of us got together to do some target shooting and check out the new shotguns some of my buddies had just bought for turkey hunting. The guns were three-inch, 12-gauge magnums with thirty-two-inch barrels.

At first they were shooting at tin cans about forty yards away, but soon they were taking shots at fifty and sixty yards. After each shot they'd rush out to count the few pellet holes in 12-ounce cans. After finding four or five holes following a fifty-yard shot one of my friends said something like "There ain't going to be a turkey safe in the woods."

Setting up a can at about sixty yards, he turned to me and said, "Hey Ray, get your old gun and see what it'll do at that range." I

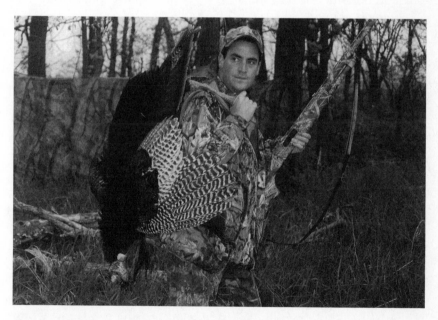

Choose a turkey gun that works well for you and the type of terrain you are hunting. A 12-gauge with a three-inch Undertaker choke and No. 6 or No. 4 shot is a good choice.

knew they were kidding me about my old humpback Browning 12-gauge that shot 2¾-inch shells.

At the time it was the gun I used for everything. I loaded it with No. 8 shot for quail and slugs for deer, and I killed quite a few turkeys with it.

I stood there and listened to my friends teasing me and insulting my gun for a while before picking up the old Browning and sliding a shell in the chamber. Standing beside my friends, I raised the gun, aimed at the far-off dot of a can and pushed off the safety. Then I quickly lowered the muzzle and blew a plate-sized hole in the dirt about ten steps away.

"See that," I said, "I never shoot a turkey much farther away than that. I do not need to shoot that far." I've seen some people buy a 10-gauge or big magnum 12-gauge for all the wrong reasons. Armed with the most powerful shotgun in America, they seem to think they can pull off superhuman shots. The result is many more wounded turkeys in the woods.

Sure, I shoot a 12-gauge magnum now, but my philosophy about range has never changed. The most important part about shooting a turkey is getting him in close for positive identification and a clean kill.

But there are some big advantages to the larger shotguns if you use them for added insurance rather than long-range artillery. The shells you shoot carry more pellets and deliver a real knockout punch when used properly.

Then again, they also have their disadvantages. For one thing, they can be pretty heavy. The extra weight may not feel like much when you're carrying it from the gun case to the car, but put in six or eight miles in rugged terrain and it's a different story.

The guns can also have punishing recoil and muzzle blast that might bother some people. Wearing good hearing protectors when you're shooting targets can make a magnum shotgun much more tolerable. Walker's Game Ear and Power Muffs are the best I've used. If you don't like the kick, then step down to a smaller gun. You can't shoot accurately if you're wincing and blinking like a toad in a hailstorm when you pull the trigger.

There's nothing wrong with using a regular 12-gauge or even a 16- or a 20-gauge if you know its limitations and don't take marginal shots.

One of the most important parts of a shotgun is the last few inches of the barrel where it's choked. If you have a gun with screw-in changeable chokes, use the tightest choke possible. Of course the choke that patterns best in your gun is the correct choice. The H.S. Undertaker turkey choke is the hands-down favorite for me and my turkey hunters.

If you are in the market for a new shotgun, the length of the barrel might be a prime consideration. Up until a few years ago it was widely believed that the longer the barrel the tighter the pattern. While this concept sounds reasonable, tests have shown barrel lengths have little effect on pattern.

The shorter barrels, say, from twenty-four to twenty-six inches have several advantages over longer lengths. One obvious plus is a slight reduction in weight. Another is handling ease; a barrel that's two feet long takes a lot less time and effort to swing and aim.

Since turkey guns are aimed rather than pointed, sights are a must for today's tight-shooting guns. If your turkey gun does not come from the factory with sights, or you're shooting an older model, there are a wide variety of good sights available. The Hi-Viz sight systems are very durable and work well for me. Low-power scopes are an option of some hunters; however, I believe the red dot sight systems are better and very effective. You shoot with both eyes open, so you see the entire target, and behind and in front of the target.

Shotgun action is largely a matter of hunter preference. Almost every action has its share of advantages and disadvantages. A single-shot is very lightweight and is the most affordable shotgun made. My brother Marty had good success with an old single-shot 20-gauge for years.

Some hunters like the fine balance and looks of a side-by-side or double-barrel, but their prices can be more than many people are willing to spend.

A semiautomatic can offer fast and accurate follow-up shots if needed and a slightly reduced recoil. The pump shotgun has probably the most versatile action on any gun. Some models sell for very reasonable prices.

Most of today's special turkey guns come in camouflage to eliminate a shiny surface that may spook turkeys. Older shotguns with the standard bluing and glossy wood can either be painted or covered with H.S. camouflage tape or a gun sock.

A sling is a great investment, making the shotgun easier to haul and freeing your hands to carry calls, cameras, and perhaps a dead turkey.

Unlike my turkey gun, which is part of my family and which I hunt with six months of the year, most turkey guns are used only a couple days a year, or a hunter borrows or buys a new gun just before the weekend hunt. Always take the time to shoot and handle your turkey gun before each season. Make sure you've handled the gun enough that it comes up smoothly and that your head just naturally nestles into the stock.

It's also good to find some woods to practice shooting from a sitting position, to simulate real hunting conditions. While you're at it, practice taking some shots from your off shoulder. Sooner or later every right-handed shooter is challenged with a bird coming in on his right.

It's much easier to simply move the gun butt a few inches rather than try to scoot your whole body around to take the shot. I've taken at least a dozen toms shooting left-handed.

TURKEY AMMUNITION

Guns and ammunition are a lot like a hunter and his dog: The little one does most of the work and the big one gets all of the credit. The shells you choose can make or break a hunt.

First, rule out using the really big shot sizes, such as No. 2 and buckshot. The large shot sizes are far more dangerous for other hunters.

And forget about using those huge loads for body shots. Trying to get a few pellets through a big gobbler's wings, feathers, breast, breast sponge, and into a bird's vitals is all but impossible.

I've seen turkeys run or fly off after being literally knocked off their feet by a body shot with goose loads. A friend once took a nice Merriam's gobbler that had two dozen No. 2 pellets buried in its breast and thighs. He killed the tom just a few days after it was wounded.

Shot sizes 4 through 7½ are the best to choose, with 4, 5, and 6 the most popular. I've always had the best success with No. 6 but some of my peers swear by No. 4. Shoot whatever patterns best in your gun.

Shells loaded with No. 7½ shot are popular with some hunters, especially at short ranges, in brushy, heavily wooded ridges where shooting a turkey at twenty feet is not uncommon. It sure makes sense if you're after a dense pattern. After all, there are well over twice as many pellets in a load of No. 7½ as compared to No. 4 shot.

The main question is whether shot that small will retain enough energy to penetrate a tom's neck or skull. The answer is yes; at normal turkey hunting ranges No. 7½ shot performs very well. Ben "Bear" Held, a good friend of mine, has been using nothing else for years, and he's built up a pretty impressive record.

Those who shoot a relatively small gun, or a gun with a modified choke, may want to take a hard look at the smaller pellets like

No. 6 or 7½. A standard 12-gauge shell loaded with No. 6 will have more pellets than a three-inch shell of No. 4. Any added pellets can also help to fill in the holes left by a modified choke.

Shotgun pellet construction can help determine how a particular load will perform. Extra-hard pellets will not only have more impact, they'll also fly truer because they won't become misshapen from the pressure of sitting in the wad and the shot. Most quality loads feature pellets that have been copper- or nickel-plated for added hardness.

Shooting a buffered load of quality shot is almost like changing to the next tightest choke at most turkey hunting ranges. That's something good to know if you're carrying a gun with a modified choke.

Generally speaking, the more powder the better for down-range penetration. There is, however, such a thing as too much powder, which brings us to the most important concept of guns and ammunition: patterning to discover what load provides the densest pattern in your gun.

Sometimes shells crammed full of powder and pellets don't pattern well. The only way you're going to know is to shoot a few shells at paper to check for pattern density. Try as many different shells as possible to see which works best from your gun.

Don't make the mistake of not being critical enough when you're patterning a load and gun. Forget about all of the skin, flesh, and wattles on a turkey. What you're aiming at is the brain and neck bone.

Most state wildlife departments offer patterning sheets that feature an x-ray view of a turkey's head and neck so that you'll know exactly where your pellets are hitting.

Start off by patterning your gun at close range, like ten to fifteen yards. Then move back in five-yard increments. You'll eventually find your gun's maximum range. Remember what it is and never

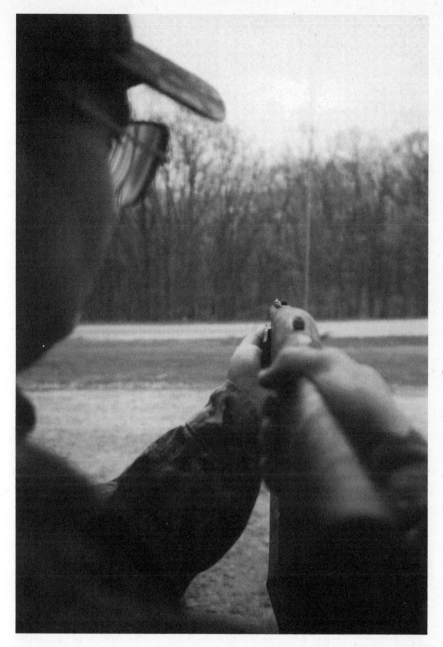

With today's tight-shooting turkey guns, sights are very important. The Hi-Viz sight system works well. Red-dot sights and low-power scopes are also good choices, depending on where you hunt.

shoot any farther. No matter what the patterning sheets tell me, I never shoot over thirty-five to forty yards in mountain timber or thick woods. I will go to heavier shot size, a good sight system and an extra-tight Undertaker choke when hunting very open farm country or on the plains of the West.

How many pellets need to strike home for the load to be good enough for hunting? Even though usually "it only takes one" I believe you need at least a dozen to insure clean kills time after time.

Once you've decided on a good load, use it as often as possible to instill confidence. Knowing that your gun/load combination can, and will, take down a gobbler will give you one less concern and slightly steadier nerves when the moment arrives.

Pattern your gun often and use the load in your turkey gun to shoot clay targets or for simple plinking. One thing for sure, today's turkey ammunition is better than ever. I'll never forget the first time I shot the then-new "turkey loads," Federal's two ounces of No. 6 shot, through my new Remington 1100 SP Magnum.

I had no patterning paper, so I stuck a soda can against a tall creek bank twenty yards away. I slipped one of the heavy shells into the chamber, rested the gun against a tree, and squeezed the trigger. My ears rang and my shoulder snapped back from the recoil.

But all the discomfort vanished when I looked at the can. It was literally demolished, looking as if it had been hit with a lawnmower. I put the gun on paper a few days later and it looked as if the target had been forced through the bottom of a sieve.

When I take a bead on a gobbler's neck at twenty to thirty yards I know exactly what's going to happen. If I do my part the gun and load will do theirs. That peace of mind more than makes up for the noise and the recoil.

Always pattern your shotgun. No. 4, 5, or 6 shot makes the best turkey loads. Find the best for your gun and the type of terrain you are hunting.

ARCHERY EQUIPMENT

Taking a big game animal with a bow and calling a turkey in so close that you can see the light in his coal-black eyes and the creases between the wrinkles on his head are two of the greatest challenges in hunting. Combine them and you have possibly the greatest accomplishment in the sport.

When a hunter uses a gun to take a turkey, the shot itself is somewhat anticlimactic. The hardest part is simply getting the bird within range. After that you try to center his head and neck in something about the size of a dinner plate.

But when you shoot with a bow, you use something that's usually less than two inches wide to hit a target that's not much bigger. Making the shot is half the battle. Consequently, there's no room for anything but the best equipment.

I've shot many turkeys with an old fifty-pound, inexpensive recurve and always felt it was more than adequate, but after switching to a sixty-five-pound custom "Shafer" recurve I discovered the advantages to shooting a really good bow with a strong draw weight. It provided the most important element—accuracy. The flatter your bow shoots the better, whether that's accomplished with stronger limbs, cams, or whatever.

Whether a hunter shoots a compound or a recurve bow with a glove or a release is up to the shooter. But I really can't overemphasize the need for the greatest accuracy. Hitting a turkey in the wrong place usually means a lost turkey. Sometimes the bird may go a long time before dying.

The main thing is to shoot a bow smoothly and comfortably. Don't use equipment if you have to give a hard yank to get to full draw. Because of the difficulty in drawing on a close bird, you'll need a bow that you can quickly and smoothly pull straight back to your anchor point.

There really isn't any need for a special turkey bow. If you're already bowhunting for deer, your current outfit will do fine. If you are thinking about getting a new compound bow, you may want to look into one of the shorter models with more let-off. You can hold full draw for a long time and shoot while sitting down. More important than the type or weight of your bow are the little things that you do to it. For one thing, you don't want even the slightest noise when making a draw. The same goes for noise at the shot. A good pro shop can show you a variety of ways to prevent such problems.

You should keep your bow well tuned so that it provides the greatest accuracy. That means having the limbs set the same. If your bow is adjustable, find out what weight produces the tightest groups.

How you camouflage a bow is largely a matter of personal preference. Many avid bowhunters carry painted bows, and some use

Hunting turkeys with a bow is quite a challenge. Practice is essential, but more important is a bow that fits you and that you are accustomed to shooting. Deer hunters can use the same bow setup for turkeys.

easily removable tape. Most new bows come out of the box in the new camouflage patterns.

Arrows should match your draw length and draw weight perfectly for optimum accuracy. Aluminum is a good choice for a flat trajectory and good penetration. Plastic vanes for fletching have the advantage of being waterproof, but many archers still carry arrows fletched with feathers. If you're new to archery, a good pro shop can save you a lot of time and money finding what's right for you and your bow.

Personally, I've always liked my arrows tipped with accurate, razor-sharp broadheads. The more cutting edge the better, as long as they fly well time after time.

There seems to be an almost endless variety of specialty products designed for archery turkey hunting. I tend to avoid most of them, but that decision rests with the shooter.

Some hunters put little washerlike stoppers on their arrows to keep them from achieving full penetration. The concept is that a turkey couldn't escape as easily with thirty inches of arrow sticking from him. Some say that the washer also provides added shock. But in my opinion nothing works better than a large-cutting-edge, very sharp broadhead accurately blown through the vitals and bone.

Using a string tracker is another popular alternative. It's simply a highly visible thread that's fastened to the arrow and attached to a spool that sits on the bow. If all goes as planned, you just follow the string to the turkey, unless he died in his tracks or flew off.

The main problems with arrow-stoppers and string-trackers are the effect they might have on accuracy and the inconvenience of using them. But don't give up even a fraction of an inch of accuracy for a little gadgetry. If you do opt for something like a string-tracker, be willing to put in the preseason hours necessary.

There's no such thing as too much shooting practice before you try to take a turkey with a bow. The vital heart/lung area, which is where I always aim, on even a mature gobbler is not much bigger than a grapefruit. You have to be both accurate and confident.

Start off shooting at very close distances, like five yards, and gradually move back. When you get to the distance at which you can't put four out of five arrows into an area the size of your fist, you're past your maximum hunting range. Few good turkey hunters will try a bow shot past twenty-five yards.

Since a turkey's kill zone is totally unlike that of most big game, it doesn't hurt to buy some targets that outline the chest cavity. If you can't find those, draw your own targets and aim for where the wings enter the body.

If you're new to hunting turkeys with a bow, try to learn as much as possible about the anatomy of a bird. Look at some dressed birds to see where the vital organs are located, then try to visualize them on every turkey photo you see.

Try to spend as much time as possible shooting under realistic conditions. Shooting judo-points in the woods at unmarked yardages while wearing your full hunting outfit can be excellent practice.

Practice from both the kneeling and standing positions. If you can figure out a way to do it when hunting, try taking shots from a sitting position as well. If you're going to be hunting from a blind of some sort, then practice shooting from it religiously.

There's one thing you can't practice for, though: how you're going to handle the excitement you feel when that big bird steps up and your bow is drawn. That's a bridge you have to cross when you come to it.

It will sure be a whole lot easier to reach the other side of that bridge if you know you're shooting good equipment very, very well.

HUNTING CLOTHES

After calls and guns, good camouflage can be a turkey hunter's most important equipment. Hunting turkeys is a game of getting an alert bird with razor-sharp eyes into close range. Good camouflage can make that much easier to accomplish.

My tastes in camouflage have changed a lot since I began hunting. Back then "camo" meant a ratty old woodland camouflage jacket, a matching hat, and a pair of faded overalls. Of course there were pants and shirts available, but getting them took money, getting money meant a job, and getting a job meant less time for calling turkeys. That idea never lasted very long.

So I made do with what I had, using good calling positions and the ability to hold stone still for whatever length of time it took to get a gobbler up close. In addition, I hunted in timbered ridges where you could not see the turkey until he was in gun range.

Choose a camouflage pattern that matches the terrain you are hunting.

But today there's too much good camouflage on the market, and a hunter is not always going to set up in a perfect place, and blending into whatever type of habitat you're hunting is imperative.

The choices in camouflage clothing seem almost endless. There are more patterns and styles available than most of us ever dreamed of just a few years ago.

As for camo patterns, there are a few key industry leaders, but there's a place for almost every camouflage on the market; just find something that matches your hunting location. There are a lot of variations across America. The deep greens and dark browns that work so well in the big woods of Dixie won't blend in on the prairies, where lighter browns and similar hues work best. If you're hunting the traditional hardwoods, a camo pattern modeled after the bark of a tree with sticks and limbs may work well.

The RealTree and Advantage patterns work very well for me and blend well anywhere in the country. Your decisions are far from over once you've picked a pattern, since there are so many styles and articles of clothing. Rely on common sense and check the quality of the clothing before you make a choice. Your decisions are far from over once you've picked a pattern, since there are so many styles and articles of clothing. Obviously the jacket is going to be your number one concern. Be sure you pick out something that's lightweight and quiet. Staying warm isn't usually a problem, but when it is, cold-weather camo today is warm but lightweight, and raingear is breathable, quiet, and comfortable. It's a good idea to select a jacket that's a little big. Some people buy a full size larger than usual so that they can move comfortably and easily. A larger jacket also allows you to dress for the weather.

As for styles, I like a coat that hangs well below my waist. Additionally, it must, and I mean absolutely must, have plenty of pockets.

Look for the same basic qualities in a pair of camouflage pants: lots of pockets and enough room for easy movement and comfort.

It sounds a little odd, but you may want to consider pants in a different color and pattern than your hunting coat. I seldom wear a matching coat and pants, because the forest floor seldom matches the trees I'm sitting against.

Many times I'll be sitting with my legs surrounded by nothing but dead leaves; so I'll wear pants with a brown leaf pattern. But don't let me make your decision. Think of what it's like where you hunt and dress accordingly.

Personally, I like a baseball-style camouflage hat for turkey hunting. It's inexpensive and fits well, and it has a long bill that can help keep the sun out of your eyes. When pulled down low it also casts a shadow over your face. Normally it's best if the pattern of your hat matches your jacket.

Muzzleloading shotguns are a great way to enjoy turkey hunting.

A good pair of camouflage gloves can help mask any inadvertent hand movement. Hunters can choose the traditional jersey glove in a couple of camouflage patterns, as well as gloves made of lightweight mesh.

I tend to opt for the jersey gloves because they fit better. I also like to cut the fingertips off for greater sensitivity when I'm working a call or gun. You'll also discover that cutting the ends off a pair of cotton gloves makes them much more comfortable in warm weather.

Nothing seems to glow in the early morning quite like a pale, uncovered face. Pulling a billed cap down low helps, as does a full beard. It's a combination I've used to call a lot of turkeys over the years. But there's no use taking chances when there are so many ways to camouflage your face. Without a doubt the most effective way is with face paints. Dabbing your face with two or three colors that match the surroundings not only helps you blend in, it's also comfortable and does nothing to impair your vision.

There are some disadvantages, however, such as the time it takes to apply and remove the makeup or the remarks you suffer when you go into a public place. It's for that reason that most hunters rely on some sort of head net or cloth to cover their faces.

There are also a variety of mesh head nets from which to choose. Hunter's Specialties has a great selection of head nets, and those are the only ones I use. My favorite face mask comes up to the bridge of my nose, covering my face but not impairing my vision. The hat pulled down low covers my forehead.

Some hunters opt for a head net that covers the entire head because they think that their eyes should be covered as well. If you take that route be sure to spend a lot of time with the net on your head so that you'll be used to looking through it. But stay out of convenience stores at four in the morning when you're wearing it.

Most face nets now have precut eyeholes for better visibility. Other good alternatives are the camouflage nets that are attached to the inside of a hunting hat. The nets do a good job of covering the face and neck, and they also store easily within the hat when not in use.

The market has also seen the introduction of several other items to help a hunter blend in, such as small clip-on leaves that hang from the coat or hat to give the camouflage a three-dimensional effect and a bit more realism.

There's actually no end to the lengths that a hunter could go to to make sure he blends into his hunting grounds. Each individual has to decide what he thinks he needs. One Ozark hunter I met was so worried that a turkey would see him smiling, and said he could not keep from smiling when the gobbler was close, so he painted his teeth green, brown, and black. (At least I think it was paint.)

The main idea is to have that ever-important total confidence in what you're wearing. But always remember that while good camouflage is very effective it is not a cure-all. No matter how well you're dressed, there's no substitute for holding still.

BOOTS

Wearing the right footwear can do a great deal to improve the success of a turkey hunt. It obviously doesn't have much effect on the birds, but it can determine whether the hunter is comfortable or miserable.

Like clothing, boots are offered in great variety, and no one boot is right for everyone. You need to consider how far you walk, the slope of the terrain, the amount of standing water, and the temperature.

One of the most important considerations is that boots fit correctly and have good ankle support. Since I cover a lot of ground, weight is also a factor. If you're walking five miles a morning, any extra ounces will feel like pounds by the time you leave the woods.

Keeping your feet dry can be difficult whether you're hunting in the dew-soaked grasslands of Kansas or in the swamps of Florida.

Materials like Gore-Tex have helped a lot. With proper care, these materials can keep you remarkably comfortable. Still, such boots weren't made for wading or extended standing in water. For that you need rubber. Rubber-bottomed boots with leather uppers still offer some good support. Full-length rubber boots are totally waterproof but aren't the most comfortable for walking.

Turkey hunting in the mountains requires a good pair of boots with nonskid soles. A boot with a waffle-style pattern on Vibram soles allows you to keep your footing where other boots might leave you sliding. Many boot companies are producing camouflage boots in a wide variety of patterns.

ACCESSORIES

There's almost no end to the list of items that could come in handy on a turkey hunt. I've listed most of the more popular equipment that some people carry. But remember this: If you head into the woods with all of these, you'll be weighed down like an overburdened pack mule.

TURKEY VEST

The turkey vest is the best thing ever invented for turkey hunting. I have and use two turkey hunting vests. The first is a Hunter's Specialties open-top lightweight vest in RealTree Hardwood. The other is Cabela's Guide Vest; it has full material over the shoulders and is worn like a jacket. I decide on which vest to use, and select the accessories dependent on terrain, weather, and the amount of walking and time spent in the woods.

FLASHLIGHT

Finding your way into the timber before daylight or leaving after dark can be much easier with a flashlight. Flashlights that use only two AA batteries are small and easy to carry, yet provide enough light for walking down a trail. The Streamlight line of lights with the green LED is my favorite.

COMPASS/G.P.S.

Some people believe carrying a compass is a sign of weakness. The way I see it, there's no strength to be gained from wandering in the wilderness for a couple of days.

I'm fortunate to have a natural sense of direction. But I've hunted with some who could get lost in the bathtub. It never hurts to take a good compass with you and to use a distinguishing landmark as a reference. You not only won't get lost, but you'll also have the confidence to cover more territory. And that often means you'll find more turkeys. The latest thing in hunting is the G.P.S. unit. Electronics is now in the hunting world. These little pocket-size units are unbelievable. You will never get lost again, and you can actually mark the location of a roosted bird so someone can go right to him.

MAP

Some hunters carry a small topographic map, especially if they don't know the area well. The maps don't prevent a hunter from getting lost as much as they help him read the lay of the land. For example, if you're on one ridge and hear a tom gobbling somewhere over another, you can check the map to see where the bird might be and how to move in on him.

BINOCULARS

A few turkey hunters on the plains and in the western mountains were the first to carry binoculars whenever they hunt. Hunters all across America now know the importance of good binoculars, which are very effective during scouting trips to open country and during the hunt. Head for the highest ground to locate feeding or displaying turkeys. Once you spot birds, close the distance and start calling.

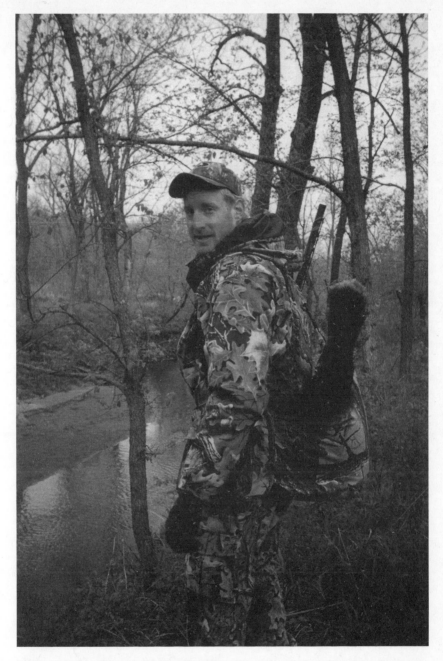

Turkey hunting vests are the greatest. They have plenty of pockets for calls, ammo, various accessories, and a turkey. Just grab your vest in the early morning and go.

EXTRA CALLS AND MATERIALS

This is something of an emergency kit I carry in the depths of my vest and never remove until needed. I always carry backup old mouth calls. With a friction call, you can never carry along too much box-call chalk or sandpaper, and always have an extra striker.

CUSHION/SEAT

Sitting on hard ground and rocks can wear a little heavy on some people's backsides. Hunters should carry a small cushion to make life more bearable. The more comfortable you are, the easier it is to sit perfectly still.

Make sure the material covering the seat blends in well with the surroundings and is relatively quiet. The cushion should also be waterproof for days when the woods are wet. The finest cushion on the market today is the Bun-Saver by H.S. and in addition they offer a small folding "strut seat" that is very comfortable, light to carry, and slightly elevates your position.

KNIFE/CLIPPERS

Most hunters always carry a knife when they enter the woods. I like to carry a small, but sturdy, folding lock-blade knife for dressing turkeys and such.

Sometimes a lightweight pair of clippers can come in handy to trim small limbs and branches near your calling site. Clippers can also enable a hunter to construct a blind much more quickly and quietly.

BLINDS

Speaking of blinds, there are some places in America where good calling sites are few and far between. A line of cottonwoods in a grazed cow pasture would offer little cover for setting up and calling.

Hunters can solve this problem with a small H. S. portable camouflage blind. They are easy to set up, and you can quickly change locations. It's important that the netting match the surroundings. Buying the material and building permanent blinds is another option. In addition there are a wide variety of pop-up blinds that completely conceal a hunter and yet are very portable.

INSECT REPELLENT

You don't know agony unless you've sat in a swamp in the Deep South, a gobbler slowly approaching while a couple of hundred mosquitoes feast on you. Even if you could move, you couldn't swat them all away, and it doesn't take long for the buzzing to drive you crazy.

At about that time you'd give a day's pay for a little quality insect repellent. In the best brands on the market a substance commonly known as DEET makes up eighty to one hundred percent of the ingredients. Only a few drops on your hands, neck, and face can discourage the likes of chiggers, ticks, and "skeeters." They can make the difference between a hunt you'll always remember and one you'd like to forget.

RAINGEAR

Spring not only brings gobbling turkeys, it also carries the threat of rain. Some hunters like to wear a lightweight, camouflage rain suit when things start getting wet. Finding a good rain suit that's quiet, well camouflaged, and comfortable enough for walking mile after mile is not a problem today. Cabela's raingear is all I wear and I never travel or hunt without it.

FLUORESCENT ORANGE

All turkey hunters should take along something that undoubtedly identifies them as human beings, and there's nothing better than fluorescent orange. Most sporting goods stores sell inexpensive vests that you can slip on while you're walking in and out of the woods, or just take your deer hunting vest and an orange hat. I carry an H.S.

blaze orange bag to put my turkey in, and I also place the bag behind my setup while calling.

CAMERA

A good camera takes up so little room yet provides so many memories. And there are so many things to be photographed, including sunrises and sunsets, pretty scenery, and special moments. Taking a picture of a bagged gobbler where he falls will always mean more than a posed shot in your garage a couple of hours later.

Hunters can buy a name-brand, automatic, 35mm camera for under a hundred dollars these days. Most are small enough to fit into a shirt pocket.

FIRST AID KIT

Most avid outdoorsmen carry a small first aid kit in their vehicles. It's also wise to put a few Band-Aids in your pocket for blisters.

ET CETERA

Like many people, by the time the sun's been up an hour or two my stomach starts rumbling even if I ate at camp. Some of the finest breakfasts I've ever tasted have been in the turkey woods while I've been working a bird.

It usually doesn't take much to hold a hunter over until lunch. Some hunters like granola bars or dried fruit mixes. My tastes are a little simpler: a couple of cookies, or better yet, a fried egg and bacon sandwich.

A small canteen of drinking water or small bottle of juice can also come in handy.

I mentioned earlier that I have two turkey vests that I always have with me. I also have additional backup products and accessories in my truck. I carry quite a bit in my vest, and I always carry extra things, like head nets and gloves for people I hunt with.

Here is a sample list of what I have in my two vests, however I may not take all of this with me at one time. It all depends on the hunt and the amount of time in the woods.

1. Twelve diaphragm mouth calls.
2. Two Wood Witch glass calls and extra strikers.
3. Two box calls.
4. Two Hammer'n crow calls.
5. H.S. Owl Hooter.
6. RealTree gloves, head net, mesh and cloth.
7. Walker's Game Ear.
8. Bun-Saver and two-way Strut Seat.
9. Blaze orange vest and safety bag.
10. Streamlight flashlights and extra batteries.
11. Hi-Viz backup sights.
12. Extra ammo, two sizes of shot, six shells in vest, three for the gun.
13. Camera and field glasses.
14. Shooting sticks.
15. Multi-tool, sharp knife, field dressing gloves.
16. Bug repellent, Bug-Out suit, raingear.
17. Compass, wet wipes, Scent-A-Way towel, toilet paper, first aid kit, extra socks.
18. Water, snacks, and when possible frozen box drinks and sandwiches.

DECOYS

The concept of a turkey decoy is pretty sound: If an approaching gobbler sees something he thinks is a hen, he'll hurry right in.

In the early years of decoys I did not care much for using them, because I put so much emphasis on good calling and calling positions. Back then, I hunted in the Ozarks, with thick woods and close-up action.

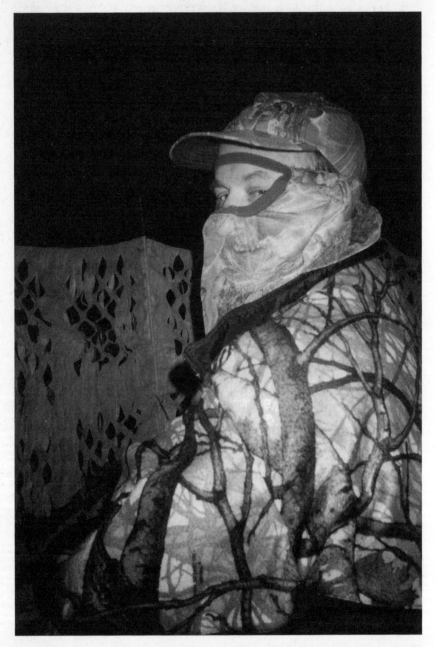

Always use a head net with eye holes. Looking through netting in dark woods impairs your vision. Face masks, gloves, good boots, and raingear all are very important.

If everything went well, the gobbler wouldn't see the decoy until he was twenty yards away, and by then he'd already be in range. In those days decoys were bulky and not the safest thing to tuck under your arm when walking through the woods.

Decoys are much better today, easy to carry, and very lifelike. Decoys work best when most hens are on the nest. Jake and gobbler decoys work because of the pecking order.

Hunters are having great success with decoys, especially those hunting more open habitats. Full-bodied decoys seem work best, but silhouettes usually get the job done too.

Hunters who are inexperienced with decoys should pay close attention to decoy placement. Decoys are not effective if you place them too far out. The gobbler may hang up twenty or thirty yards away from the decoy, or even farther—to display and wait for the hen to make the next move. Set your decoys so the turkey will pass you on his way to the artificial sweetheart. A right-handed shooter

Glassing for turkeys during scouting and hunting is part of today's turkey hunting.

The ATV is a valuable tool in today's turkey hunting. It's great transportation for hunters, scouting, crossing streams, getting through miles of mud, placing blinds, and hauling television crews and equipment.

Decoy placement is important. Always place decoys in a field edge or clearing. Hen decoys work best when hens are on the nest. During early seasons the jake or gobbler decoy is effective.

should set up on a field edge so the gobbler's approach is from the right, and should set the decoys off to the left and only out around twenty yards.

Use great caution when using a decoy. I recommend that the decoys face directly away from you in a field or clearing so that the full image is at your side. Stay a few trees back in the timber and watch and listen for other hunters sneaking in. Keep the decoy covered or draped in fluorescent orange as you move from place to place.

24

HUNTING SAFETY

In my opinion it is really a shame that we have to discuss safety in the same sentence with turkey hunting. I understand the importance of gun safety anytime we handle firearms. I was taught at a very early age to respect firearms. Treat every gun as if it was loaded; never ever take the safety off until your target was positively identified. You did not point a gun at anything you were not going to shoot. While hunting you could not shoot a game animal unless you were absolutely sure it was legal, and you took only the best possible shot to take it cleanly. Yes, respect for wildlife is also important.

In my entire life I have never seen another hunter who looked like a legal turkey. But mistaken-for-game shootings do happen, and unsafe gun handling does result in accidents every season. But remember one thing: turkey hunting, per one hundred thousand participants, is safer than football, bass fishing, tennis, swimming, or horseback riding. Like anything else, there are just a few hunters by whom all others are judged.

It all seemed so perfect for my friend Arlon Held. He'd located a gobbler and closed the distance to the bird. His calling position was perfect, and the bird was gobbling and on the way.

Arlon's gun was up and he was scanning the woods in front of him for the gobbler that should show up at any second. Arlon was being cautious, moving only his eyes, and listening for any telltale hints of the approaching turkey.

The next sound he heard was far from what he was expecting. A loud roar boomed from his right, and his head jerked sharply to the left. Momentarily stunned, he soon figured out just what had happened: Someone had shot at him. It wasn't an accidental discharge, either. Someone had aimed a gun at him and pulled the trigger.

He lay on the ground and screamed, partly out of fear and partly out of pure anger, for several minutes. The person who had pulled the trigger never showed himself. He never even checked to see if Arlon was seriously injured.

By a weird but fortunate quirk of fate, Arlon wasn't hurt, but the top of his camouflage hat was literally blown open. An old stump a few feet to his right had saved him. It had taken the brunt of the load and it was ravaged with shot.

A knot still settles in my stomach when I think about that stump not being there to take that load of shot. Had Arlon been sitting even an inch or two more erect, that could have been his last turkey hunt, or last anything for that matter.

I wish I could say that Arlon is the only one of my friends who's been through such an ordeal, but he's not. Some haven't shared his "luck." What a shame that people are so negligent they would shoot at another hunter.

And I'll never understand it. I've seen thousands of turkeys and thousands of men, and I've never seen a man who looked like a turkey. There's no excuse for confusing the two, especially in the spring when the hunter should see a visible beard before firing.

But unfortunately there are some who lose sight of what turkey hunting is about. They have to kill a turkey at all costs. They see it almost as a rite of manhood and a quick and easy way to be a hero.

In a sporting goods store the night before a new season I've seen the gleam in someone's eye and heard the fever in his voice as he buys a new magnum shotgun and talks about "blowing one away."

Imagine how such a person is going to hunt. He wants a turkey so badly that every sound he hears will be interpreted as the gobbler of his dreams. He wants a turkey so badly that in his mind he sees a bird when he pulls the trigger on another human.

And what's to be done? Some have called for mandatory fluorescent orange clothing. But to me that's attacking the problem from the wrong side. The answer lies in education. Most game departments go to great lengths to teach the ways of safe turkey hunting. But safe turkey hunting rests in the hands of each individual who participates in the sport.

Don't ever think it can't happen to you, that you can't get shot or shoot someone. Take no chances.

Done correctly, turkey hunting is a sport in which the hunter sits and the bird comes to him. With that in mind, neither I nor my clients or friends ever load our guns until we're set up and calling.

Your chances of walking up on a gobbler and getting a shot are slim to none anyway. Your odds are the same for stalking within range of what might be a calling turkey. Never sneak in on hen yelps. First of all, you're after bearded gobblers, and even if the hen does have a tom with her, you'll probably never get close enough for a shot. And if those calls are coming from a hunter you could be mistaken for a turkey . . . or worse.

Whenever you even think you hear another hunter working a bird, stay completely out of the area. No wild turkey is worth taking a chance on you or someone else getting hurt.

Yelping on a call while walking through the woods can be another accident waiting to happen. Countless times every year, some guy with a gun and a license hears turkey calls coming down a trail. His adrenaline takes the place of caution, he sees movement, and—bang!

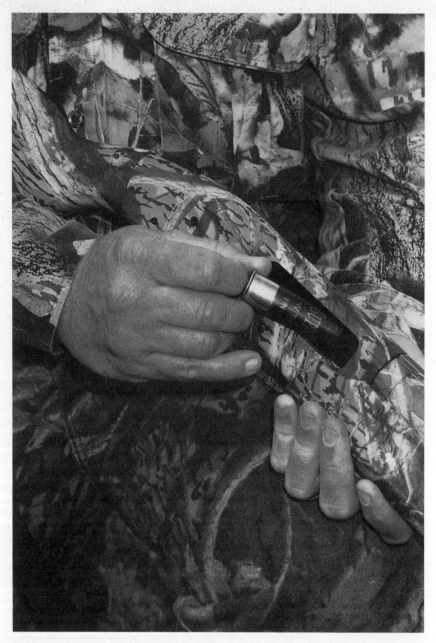

Some hunters load guns in the dark at the truck and walk into the dark woods. Never load your gun until you are set up in a calling position. And when you move to a new location, always unload the gun.

A hunter walking through the woods or a field behind another hunter should always carry the gun backwards.

Now you realize why many experienced turkey hunters wear fluorescent orange when moving through the woods. When calling, they place the fluorescent orange behind their calling tree to warn hunters coming from the rear.

Don't call until you're fully set up. It's also a good idea to sit still and spend a few minutes listening and looking for signs of other hunters. Make sure you're fully camouflaged. Make sure you're not wearing any visible white, red, blue, or black which could be confused with the color of a gobbler.

As you sit, interpret each sound as that of an approaching hunter. Move only your eyes as you scan the woods. Even when you have a bird gobbling and coming and you know he's close, make sure it's not a man before you raise your gun. Several times I've had hunters suddenly materialize up over a rise, to replace a spooked gobbler that was right there one minute earlier.

You may hope that it never happens, but it will. There will come a day when you're set up and you look out and see him—a hunter heading your way. He may have stumbled on you quite by accident or he may be coming to your calls. If the latter is the case, he may be stalking you, moving slowly with his gun ready and his finger on the trigger.

I've been there many times, and it's scary as hell. All thoughts of turkeys instantly vanish as some guy with a loaded gun and a wild look on his face approaches your setup.

Whatever you do, don't make any turkey sounds. Don't draw any subtle attention to yourself: no whistling, no raised hands, no movement of any kind.

Let the other hunter know there's a person in the area. Don't yell "hey" or some profanity. (Not yet, anyway.) Loudly and firmly say something unmistakably human, such as "Good morning!" or "Nice day, isn't it!" Even after you've spoken out loud, don't take anything for granted. Hold perfectly still until you're absolutely sure the guy knows you're a person. Even if it's someone trespassing on your private honey hole, keep calm and take your time. Only when you see that the "hunter" is relaxed and has his gun down do you show yourself.

Experienced hunters must teach safety procedures to newcomers.

Another tactic works for me, and I have used this many times. I sing some stupid song really loud. That works well. The approaching hunter knows you're there and will usually leave very quickly. You do not have to discuss anything with him, and have more time to find another turkey.

Hunters are mistaken for game while carrying a dead bird flopping over their shoulder through the woods. After you shoot a turkey, wrap it in an orange vest or put it in one of the specially designed blaze orange carrying bags from H.S. Most new turkey vests will hold a turkey and have blaze orange that snaps to the outside of the vest.

But there are reasons for accidents other than being mistaken for game. Pure carelessness could have cost me when I stupidly let an excited young client crawl behind me with a loaded gun. The magnum load of No. 4 shot plowed a yard-long furrow not four inches from my legs.

I hope I haven't scared anyone away from turkey hunting. The sloppy hunters who shoot at other hunters really are a very small minority. Chances are, you'll hunt all your life with no problems.

But please be aware that accidents can happen to ordinary people like you. Ask my friend Arlon. He'll tell you that accidents can happen.

Safe gun handling is no accident; today's hunter safety programs are very successful throughout the country. Education is the key to reducing hunting accidents. As a turkey hunter, you must do your part, so you and everyone you hunt with will have great time and a safe turkey hunting season.

25

MEMORABLE GOBBLERS

EUGENE

I first met Eugene early in the spring of 1983, during a preseason scouting trip to the hills where I was raised. I'd been walking the maze of old logging roads that laced the hardwoods, stopping occasionally to hoot or maybe hen call to pinpoint gobblers.

But the gobble that came from that long, high glade was like no other. It was . . . well, powerful. When that bird opened up every other turkey within hearing distance grew silent. When I came back to scout the next time, and the next, and the next, that bird was always on the same glade. His loud, rattling gobble had begun to get a hold on me.

I named him Eugene after a fat, smart-mouthed kid I knew in grade school who wouldn't utter a peep when he was close to you. But let him get across the playground where you couldn't get to him and he'd call you every name in the book.

Eugene the turkey was the same way.

He'd stand out near the lip of that glade where he could see for dozens of miles and gobble and gobble at every hoot, crow call, and hen call—as long as I kept my distance. But when I sneaked to the back side of the glade to call, he wouldn't so much as cluck. You'd swear he had disappeared.

Yet when I got to where I could view the glade, I'd see him standing there, as big as a potbellied stove. He'd stare me in the eye for a few seconds before sailing off into the valley.

He became an obsession with me. I didn't really want to kill him as much as I wanted to fool him. I studied him every chance I got, and a couple of times before the season I called him within good camera range.

This gobbler was big, probably bigger than any turkey I've ever seen. It was obvious he'd been in these hills for years. I have one slide of him strutting away from the camera that shows a pair of spurs as long and as thick as flint arrowheads.

I'll never know if Eugene was just plain smart or just plain lucky, but something kept him out of shotgun range.

The first day I was really able to work Eugene during the season, I had a partner with me, a gentleman with failing health. A two-hundred-yard walk from the truck was for him a major hike. By the time I got the big gobbler fired up my hunter was totally exhausted.

We did our best to set up in a small tangle of limbs and vines, the only available cover. The woods were open that year, and Eugene got suspicious the minute he stepped onto the opposite end of the flat. He ended up circling to the other side of the hollow and staring straight across at us. I swear he was enjoying it.

A few days later, Max Shekelton and I set out at midmorning to give Eugene a try. He was on his glade as usual, but today he had some hens and another gobbler fairly close by.

We set up, and Eugene gobbled at everything, as did the other gobbler. The two toms were soon so fired up that Max and I could hear the excited purrs, pops, and thumps of a full-scale gobbler fight.

One of the turkeys finally flew off and the winner let out a victorious gobble—it was Eugene. I hit him with everything I knew, even trying to get his hens fired up, but nothing worked.

Max and I decided to go after the gobbler that had just left. It took some doing, but he finally came in and Max got him. It was tough to believe that the bird had come out second best.

Max's gobbler weighed 23½ pounds, and had a 12-inch beard and spurs that were exactly 1½ inches long. But he had been beaten bad. His plumage was raked and his breast was scarred with deep gouges from Eugene's spurs.

I took a couple of clients back after Eugene a couple of days later. He wouldn't come in to calls, but I could get him to follow me as I backed out. One hunter passed up a shot he thought was too far. Afterwards we stepped off the distance and found it a little over thirty yards. Eugene had lucked out again.

That same morning I tried to pull another fast one on Eugene. Since he was starting to walk away gobbling whenever I moved in, I decided to circle him and push him toward my hunters.

I cut my circle and hooted once to find the bird's location. He gobbled from not thirty yards away, stepped into the logging road strutting, and then flew off.

The last day of the season was greeted by a gully-washing rain that flooded many roads. But my brother Marty and I took Verle Pemberton and Jim Toby, a pair of very good hunters, into the woods after Eugene. We worked in and around Eugene's glade most of the morning.

Marty finally got a trio of gobblers calling and coming in. He could tell by the gobbles that Eugene wasn't among them, but any gobbler's a good gobbler when there's only an hour left in the season.

The three toms came up, and Jim Toby dropped the lead bird of twenty-one pounds. Just a split second before Jim pulled the trigger, Marty noticed movement to his right. It was Eugene, easily towering a foot above the other turkeys. Marty swung his gun but Eugene ducked, ran, and flew off into the rain.

That was the last time we saw him. He wasn't there the next spring. And for some reason, turkey hunting in those hills hasn't been the same since.

THE TOMBIGBEE GOBBLER

There are times when a turkey hunter has no choice but to buck the odds and try to accomplish what is widely known as the improbable, if not the impossible. I've always held to the theory that a hunter should go for it when he has nothing to lose. He who does is often surprised at what a gobbler might do when he really wants to.

Ben Held and I had gone to Alabama for some seminars and calling contests, but more importantly for some turkey hunting. I've always rated the easterns of Alabama as some of the toughest turkeys in America. Even though there are lots of them, getting one in front of a gun is a challenge for the best of hunters.

That particular day the challenge seemed especially tough.

Ben and I were the guests of David Crowe and his brother, Bob. We were hunting a good-looking stretch of woods and fields that bordered the Tombigbee River. The problem was that the habitat was equally good on the other side of the river, and that was where the turkeys were. We fanned out and hunted our side of the river hard, but by midmorning all that was left to do was call to turkeys across the river. I had one bird on the other side eating out of my hand; he was gobbling at everything. But prospects didn't look good with two hundred yards of water between us.

As I lay there in the grass, I thought back to all the times I'd seen gobblers flying across rivers in the Ozarks. Though the Ozark rivers were small compared to the Tombigbee, I'd seen a lot of turkeys sail across them as if it was an everyday event. Surely these Alabama birds did the same thing. After all, our side of the river had been full of turkeys the day before, and I doubted that they'd put on swim fins or chartered a ferry.

Comparing mental notes on all of the birds I'd seen back home, I realized that turkeys seemed to cross at favored places. Maybe these Alabama birds did the same. I grabbed my gear and went on a quick scouting mission.

Sure enough, I found a small sandbar downstream that melted into open woods. It was absolutely covered with turkey tracks. At first I thought this might be a place where the birds went to water. Checking closer, I saw several big gobbler tracks that simply disappeared at the water's edge.

I backed up into the nearby trees and started calling. The bird I'd worked earlier was still fired up. I could hear the bird getting closer and closer to the river's far bank. Finally I could see him strutting back and forth on a small sandbar across from me.

Figuring I had nothing to lose I poured the calls to him. I admit to being more than a little surprised when he dropped out of strut, took a few steps, and sailed across the river toward me.

The turkey landed amid the tracks on the sandbar in front of me, gobbled, and went into strut. I called and he folded up and headed my way.

To this day I don't know what I did, but somehow I spooked that bird and he headed back toward the river. I tried a shot with the muzzleloader I was carrying, but hit only the air where the turkey had been.

David Crowe had been close enough to hear the whole thing. We agreed it was a special accomplishment to have gotten the bird across the water; it would have been just a little nicer if I'd had the bird to show for it.

We were back on the same property the next morning. Aside from a gobbler that we spooked off his roost, all of the birds still seemed to be on the other side of the river.

Figuring I still had nothing to lose, I headed to the place where I'd missed the chance of a lifetime the day before. This time I decided to set up closer to the sandbar. As for calls, I used old reliable — my voice.

A gobble sounded from the place where I'd started the bird the day before. I increased my intensity, and the bird responded some more. To make a long story short, I ended up calling nearly nonstop for close to forty-five minutes. The bird came to within three hundred yards of the river's edge, where he strutted back and forth, gobbling with almost every breath. Growing hoarse, I sent one last series of excited cutting across to the bird.

The gobbler flapped his wings and went into a glide that brought him to the same spot on the sandbar he'd flown to yesterday. He shook himself off and stepped up onto the riverbank. I got it right the second time.

David Crowe was on the scene in seconds. He'd been set up where he could see the whole thing.

We'll never know for sure if that was the same longbeard I'd called across and missed the day before. But the bird had responded the same, had come from the same spot, and had even looked the same.

THE CONFUSED MERRIAM'S

Just when you think you're really starting to understand turkeys, you happen across one that leaves you totally dumbfounded. I'm not talking about birds that are super shy and seemingly impossible to call. I'm talking about turkeys that seem, well, crazy.

I met such a bird the first day I ever hunted the Merriam's of South Dakota's Black Hills. It was an afternoon hunt and I was guiding a gentleman from Minnesota for John Hauer. A third hunter tagged along.

John dropped us off in some of the prettiest turkey country I'd ever seen. Rolling hills of ponderosa pines lay separated by small meadows. A gin-clear little stream bisected the property.

The shadows were stretching far across the meadow when I got a bird to gobble at my version of an elk bugle that I made with a triple-reed diaphragm. We hurried across a big open field and over a fence as we tried to get to the bird before he flew up to roost.

I made some hen calls at the edge of the timber where the bird had gobbled. Nothing. I tried again. Still nothing. I tried another elk bugle and a bird gobbled, but the sound came from the area we'd just left. "We might as well go roost him for the morning," I told the client.

As we stepped out of the timber I looked up and there, not thirty steps from where I'd bugled the first time, was a turkey. Even at close to 350 yards you could tell it was a big old gobbler in strut. I made some loud hen calls, but the bird showed no response.

Since this was the client's first turkey hunt I decided to bugle again so that the client could use his binoculars to watch a turkey gobble. I bugled, the bird gobbled, and then he took off on a dead run—right at us!

I hen called again, and the bird slowed to a walk. When I followed with a bugle, he gobbled and came at us full speed.

There we were, three of us standing in the open, with basically nothing but three hundred yards of open field between us and a kamikaze turkey. When the gobbler dropped from sight in a slight gully, the three of us hurried to a scraggly stand of trees fifty yards away.

The gobbler had slowed a bit when he came back into view. Trying to hurry him along, I hit him with aggressive hen calls and he slowed even more. "Bugle again," somebody said. I did, and the bird gobbled hard and broke into a sprint, coming right at us. I never hen called to that Merriam's again.

"This isn't exactly your normal turkey hunt," I told the novice from Minnesota. There we were, sitting in the middle of a few spindly pines surrounded by nothing but grass and wildflowers, being charged by some elk-hating turkey. To top it off, it was nearly too dark to shoot.

The bird continued at us on a dead run, his long beard swinging like a pendulum back and forth in front of his chest. Things looked good; the client had his gun up and was holding as steady as a rock.

But when the gobbler was seventy yards out he saw the third member of our party. Still the turkey kept coming, now angling a little to our right but still approaching on a dead run. Nothing I could do would stop him.

When he passed by, we took our best shot. Unscathed, the gobbler never broke stride or showed any alarm. He continued on across the meadow and disappeared into the pines behind us.

It just goes to show: There's no figuring turkeys.

26

HUNTERS I HAVE KNOWN

FRANCIS

Most of the hunters a person meets while guiding are fine people. Over the years I've been fortunate to have guided people from all walks of life. Many have become cherished friends.

But every once in a while I get someone like Francis. Francis had booked a spring hunt and showed a lot of enthusiasm, calling me weekly to make sure the hunt was on. He showed up a half hour early the morning of the hunt.

You could tell by his lily-white skin and brand new hunting clothes that Francis was something of a stranger to the outdoors. But he was exceptionally pleasant and eager. We loaded up my Jeep and took off.

When we got atop the ridge I wanted to hunt, Francis pulled a shiny Remington 1100 out of a case. I mean you could tell by the looks and smell of the gun that it was fresh out of the box and un-fired. Next he reached for a box of three-inch magnum shells, wrapping his manicured fingers around the first layer of the box.

The next time I looked, there was Francis, shells in one hand, shotgun in the other, and a very puzzled look on his face as he glanced from one to the other. "Excuse me," he finally said, "could you please tell me where the bullets go?"

"Sure," I replied. Opening a pocket on my coat, I said, "How about the bullets go right here until we need them."

It was the kind of morning guides usually see only in their dreams. The birds gobbled hard on the roost and didn't quiet throughout the morning.

Francis and I started the morning setting up about 150 yards from a gobbler that was sounding off like a broken record. I gave the bird a few soft yelps. He flew down and hit the ground gobbling.

It was about then that the gobbler and a smaller tom walked into view. "Hey, it looks like there's two of them," Francis said loudly, obviously proud that he could see them.

Being a little loud was a problem that would plague Francis throughout the day. He traversed the Ozark hills with all the finesse of a man dragging a ball and chain—on each foot. Each time we'd begin to move in on a bird, he'd spook it.

Then I came up with a scheme I thought would surely work. At the head of a hollow I stopped, turned to Francis, and whispered, "We have to really be quiet when we're walking through this area . . . ridgegators."

"Ridgegators?" Francis questioned. "Yeah," I said, "they're kind of like alligators with hooved feet and they live up in these hills. They're real tough to see because they have a dead-leaf pattern on their backs. They just hold real still and when they hear a mouse or squirrel running through the leaves they snap out and grab it."

"Really?" Francis asked. "Yeah, but sometimes they'll snap at anything rustling in the leaves," I continued. "I had a client making too much noise up here last week and *snap!* It looked like he'd sat on an open blender."

My plan worked. Francis moved through the woods as quiet as a feather in the wind.

We were sneaking down an old logging trail when a gobbler answered one of my hoots. The bird was close enough that I could hear the rattle in his gobble, and I guessed he was just off the lip of the ridge maybe sixty yards away.

I whispered for Francis to sneak up to an old oak in front of me, handed him a "bullet," and told him to shoot the bird in the face as soon as he saw a beard.

Francis sneaked to the oak without so much as rustling a leaf. When he was all set, he carefully placed the shell in the gun's chamber. Then with a single finger he pushed the little silver button that forced the action home with a crash that echoed down the hollow.

Looking over the top of his pop-bottle-thick glasses, Francis turned to me and whispered, "O.K., Ray, call that S.O.B. up." We hunted the rest of the morning but couldn't get Francis a shot at a bird.

After we left the woods we stopped at a little country tavern for a cheeseburger and beer and to see how other hunters had fared. The place got kind of quiet when my obviously misplaced friend and I walked up to the bar and straddled a couple of stools.

Things eventually picked back up in the bar. People started talking, and the sounds of turkey calls floated throughout. You could see Francis starting to feel more at ease. Finally, doing his best to fit in, Francis turned to the old stubble-faced backwoodsman sitting beside him, slid the hat back on his balding head and said, "Boy, the damn ridgegators are really bad this year, ain't they?"

THE COW AND THE GOBBLER

Down in southern Missouri there used to be an old gobbler that roosted up on a ridge where a farmer, a half-crazy old bachelor, swore he'd shoot anybody caught hunting on his place.

Every morning the gobbler would sail off the roost and land in the middle of a huge pasture, calling to hens as he stood out there and strutted among the Herefords. The owner of the pasture let most of the locals hunt, and almost everybody had given the tom a try.

Hunters would set up on the edge of the pasture and try to call, but the bird wouldn't ever budge. People tried decoys, hen calling, gobbling, and jake yelping, but nothing made any difference; the gobbler wouldn't move.

Hunters even tried sneaking to the field's edge, hoping to get a shot at the gobbler as he left the field, but the bird always managed to fly from the center of the field untouched.

Every day of the season someone would stop at the local cafe with a tale of frustration at trying to kill that turkey. Finally a couple of hunters in our camp, Mark and H.D., came up with what they said would be a sure-fire—and legal—way to kill that old gobbler. Bets and wagers started flying, with all the locals swearing that old tom just couldn't be killed.

That night I pulled Mark aside and asked him about his plan. Heck, I may not be the best turkey hunter in the world but I've called in more than my share of turkeys and I knew that bird had made a fool out of me and everyone in the county who owned a turkey call.

Mark explained that he and H.D. had made themselves a red and white cow suit. They knew that the gobbler wasn't spooked by cows, and they figured they'd just ease out into the field and put the hurt on him.

Mark and H.D. were at the edge of the cow pasture long before dawn the next morning with the cow suit in two pieces. Mark was to take the front piece while H.D. brought up the rear. When they got close enough to the gobbler they'd slide a shotgun out the peephole Mark was using, and the gobbler, as well as the bets, would be theirs.

Sure enough, at first light the gobbler gobbled a couple of times on the roost and sailed down to the middle of the pasture. Mark and H.D. started easing out into the field, H.D. holding the stock of the shotgun while Mark held the barrel and acted as the cow's eyes.

All bent over and unable to see, H.D. kept asking Mark about their position. "Where's he at?" H.D. asked. "He's still about seventy yards out," Mark whispered. "I don't want to head right at him. Let's just take our time and get closer."

They moved slowly and easily; first Mark took a step and then H.D. took a step to catch up. Another ten minutes passed and H.D. said, "How we doing? Let's hurry and make him a jellyhead so I can get out of this suit and straighten up."

"Just be patient," said Mark. "He's about forty-five yards out and I think it's going to work. He's totally ignoring us. Just fifteen more yards and we'll smoke him."

The cloth cow steadily inched across the pasture. Suddenly Mark stopped in his tracks and H.D. slammed into his back. "Why'd you stop?" H.D. asked.

"There's a bull looking at us," said Mark. "Don't worry about that damn bull," H.D. said. "I don't care about any old bull. Keep moving so we can double-team that turkey."

Mark started off again but stopped when they were just out of gun range. H.D. slammed into his back again. "What's wrong this time?" H.D. asked.

"Uh-oh, that bull I told you about, he's hurrying this way with a strange look in his eye," said Mark.

"What are we going to do?" H.D. asked.

Mark said, "Well, I'm going to act like I'm eating some grass, but you'd better brace yourself."

STORE-BOUGHT YELPER

Being the kind of kid I was, the kind that drove my family crazy with nonstop talk of turkey hunting, I somehow got passed off onto Uncle Lee. The patient soul he was, good old Uncle Lee always had time to talk hunting with me and to make sure I got out during the season. He also introduced me to some of the most colorful characters I've ever met.

Old Joe was one of Lee's closest hunting buddies. About as Ozark as you could get, Joe always wore a brown toothy smile across a face that was usually covered with a tobacco-stained stubbly beard. No one knew for sure if old Joe either didn't know how to tie his boots or was just too lazy to do so. He did manage to zipper his pants about half of the time, though.

One afternoon Uncle Lee and I were in his yard when Joe's '53 Chevrolet pickup truck came barreling onto the property. You could see Joe's ear-to-ear smile despite the cobwebs of cracks that covered his windshield.

He got out of his truck and proudly boasted that he had a brand new, store-bought mouth yelper. Now we'd seen mouth calls before, but they'd always been made of plumber's lead and a condom from the men's room down at the gas station.

"Looky here," said Joe. "I'm gonna be the very first turkey hunter in Iron County to kill hisself a turkey with a fancy store-bought mouth call."

"Well, what's it sound like?" asked Uncle Lee.

"I ain't opened it yet but it'll sound real good," said Joe. "It says right here on the back all you do is put it in your mouth, put your tongue on the call, blow air, and it's guaranteed to make all the calls of the wild turkey."

"I don't know," said Uncle Lee. "I think you might want to do some practicing on it." Joe just scoffed at the idea and shoved the package into his pocket.

Joe's old Chevy rolled into Lee's driveway about four the next morning, the opening day of turkey season. We could see Joe inside his cab, using a cigarette lighter to read and reread the instructions for the call, which was still in its package.

We drove up an old logging road to the top of the mountain behind my grandma's house. When Uncle Lee and I left Joe, he was walking out onto an open glade and just getting out his knife to take the mouth yelper out of its wrapping.

Uncle Lee and I headed down the ridge just as it began to get light. The songbirds were starting to sing, and the whole woods was beginning to wake up as a light orange color spread across the east.

At about that time we heard a great horned owl hoot in the distance. Then a turkey gobbled. Shortly thereafter, another turkey gobbled down near the place where we'd last seen Joe.

And then we heard it. A low, grunting kind of gagging cough came from the same general area. "What was that, Uncle Lee?" I asked. "I'm not exactly sure," answered Lee.

Lee waited a few moments, then hooted like a barred owl, and a turkey gobbled just down the ridge. Then we heard that terrible gagging sound again, only this time it was louder and deeper. "I sure hope that's not Joe dying," said Uncle Lee. "We'd better go check."

When we got to him, Joe was sprawled out on his hands and knees. Sweat was pouring from his pale white face and he was gasping for air. Uncle Lee put his hand on Joe's shoulder and said, "My God, Joe, are you all right? I tried to tell you that you should've tried using that thing before we got into the woods. Look at you, it's gobbling time! Are you going to make it?"

Joe looked up, tears running down his cheeks, and said, "I, I, I think I swallered it."

"Swallowed it, are you sure?" asked Uncle Lee.

"I think so," said Joe. "I've been through three piles of puke and haven't found it yet."

27

THE FUTURE OF TURKEY HUNTING

Most hunters would agree that there's something special about wild turkey hunting. It's the kind of sport that, once tried, is seldom abandoned. You're hooked for life.

Youth hunts like this one are vital for educating and involving today's young people in turkey hunting.

But turkey hunting can't continue on its own. Just as all hunting needed help a half a century ago, today's turkey hunting is going to need a lot help in the next fifty years as well. Every year we see more and more factors threatening the sport that is so important to us. Things such as loss of habitat and groups supporting unrealistic concepts of wildlife management, wacko animal rights extremists, and gun laws are very real threats to absolutely every sportsman and to hunting as we know it today.

We ask that all hunters join such organizations as the National Wild Turkey Federation, the National Rifle Association, and other pro-hunting associations. It's important that sportsmen not only join, but that they get involved as well, donating both time and money.

We can't survive by complaining among ourselves. Hunters must take an active stand, writing letters to politicians and government agencies. Just as importantly, we need to police our own ranks,

David Eye, the author's youngest son, with his second Missouri gobbler.

Marty Eye and his son Cody on a successful youth turkey hunt.

work with hunter and gun safety education programs, as well as improving landowner–sportsman relations.

We almost lost turkey hunting once, but we were lucky enough to get it back through a lot of hard work. If we lose it again we probably won't get another chance.

We hope you'll help preserve what we so enjoy for the future. Good luck, and safe hunting.

Ray Eye

The U.S. Sportsmen's Alliance
801 Kingsmill Parkway
Columbus, Ohio 43229
(614) 888-4868
www.ussportsman.org

National Rifle Association
11250 Waples Mill Road
Fairfax, VA 22030-7400
1-800-672-4868
www.nra.org

The National Wild Turkey
Federation
770 Augusta Road
P.O. Box 530
Edgefield, SC 29824-0530
www.nwtf.org

INDEX

Coyote calls, example, 77, 79
Coyote howlers, 62
Coyotes, problems with, 85–86
Crow calls, 62
  example, 77
  using, 83–84, 87, 90
Crowe, Bob, 230
Crowe, David, 130, 230–32
Cushion, 210
Cutting
  box call, 78
  diaphragm calls, 56
  hens, 27–28
  with slate, 48
  toms, 31
  use, 114, 115

D
Dawn, importance of, 83–87
Dawn scatter, flock, 116
Decoys, 213–17
  full-bodied, 215
  placement, 215–17
Depth perception, sitting, 101
Diaphragm call, 39, 44, 51, 54–60
  care, 60–61
  instructions, 58–60
  material, 55
  photo, 60
  sizing, 57–58
  storage, 61
Doctor Doom, photo, 161
Double-barrel shotgun, 192
Double-reed calls, 44, 56, 57
Drinking water, 212

Droppings
  scouting, 66, 67
  size, photo, 68
Dusting bowls, scouting,
    photo, 71

E
Eastern Wild Turkey, 12, 13
  nest, photo, 23
  photo, 12
Education, and involvement of
    youth, 243
Elk bugle, 62
  using, 233
Equipment, 187–217
Eugene, author's turkey
    experience, 227–30
Evolution, 9, 11
Experimenting, with calling, 41,
    49, 60, 136
Eye, Cody, photo, 245
Eye, David, photo, 244
Eye, Marty, 166, 192, 229
  bowhunting, 177–79
  photos, 173, 174, 181, 245

F
Face
  camouflage, 205
  cover, 205–6
Facenets, 205–6
Fall gobblers, 166–77
  photos, 161, 168, 172, 173, 174
Fall hunting, 155–75
  calling, 169